THE
ENNEAGRAM
for the spirit

BARRON'S

THE
ENNEAGRAM
for the spirit

Mary Horsley

First edition for the United States and Canada published
in 2005 by Barron's Educational Series, Inc.

First published in Great Britain in 2005 by Gaia Books, an
imprint of Octopus Publishing Group, 2–4 Heron Quays,
London, E14 4JP

All inquiries should be addressed to:
Barron's Educational Series, Inc.
250 Wireless Boulevard
Hauppauge, New York 11788
http://www.barronseduc.com

International Standard Book Number 0-7641-3195-8
Library of Congress Catalog Card No. 2004112283

Printed in China

9 8 7 6 5 4 3 2 1

contents

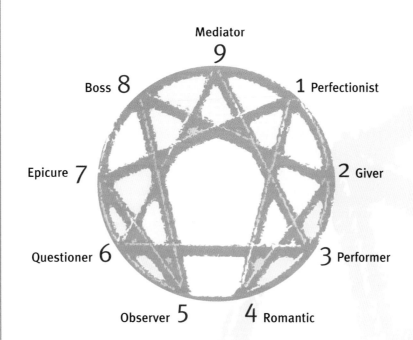

Mediator 9

Boss 8

1 Perfectionist

Epicure 7

2 Giver

Questioner 6

3 Performer

Observer 5

4 Romantic

a note from the author

It's only when we truly know and understand that we have a limited time on earth – and that we have no way of knowing when our time is up – that we will begin to live each day to the fullest, as if it was the only one we had.

Elisabeth Kubler-Ross

I have been involved in the field of personal development for most of my adult life, starting with working with small children who were homeless in the East End of London in the 1960s. Ironically I was myself rehoused as homeless with my two small children when I began my yoga training in the late 1970s. I taught yoga for many years and studied to be an acupuncturist with the charismatic J. R. Worsley in the five-element technique during the early 1980s, and later went on to further studies in acupuncture at Guangzhou College of Traditional Chinese Medicine in China. Having grown up the daughter of a most unusual doctor – vegetarian, mystic, and anti-vivisectionist – I was always aware that we need to take responsibility for our own health, both physical and emotional, and for our own lives. Surviving a near-fatal attack of malaria in my early thirties illuminated this point.

Not long after this, in 1984, I was introduced to the Enneagram when I met one of its chief exponents in the USA – psychologist and psychic Helen Palmer, who was a friend of my American fiancé. She had spent much of the 1960s helping Vietnam War draft dodgers slip across the border into Canada, and they met while he was evading the authorities. Their conversation was perplexing. It went something like this: "Yes, well, he is a Nine, he's not at all clear about where it goes next." Or: "He just wants me to stand up and fight; match his Eight." Clearly, if I was going to keep up I was going to have to learn their language.

I was given a large pile of photocopied material originating from Helen and her group of Enneagram exponents from Berkeley, California, describing nine distinct personality types. She was yet to shape it into her first book, *The Enneagram, the Definitive Guide to the Ancient System for Understanding Yourself and the Others in Your Life*.

I read through the material absolutely fascinated. It was as if I had been handed the key to the universe. Characters from my world leapt out of the pages. The myth that we are all basically alike was exploded or, rather, rewritten. The nine types are alike. Put a panel of six or seven Ones on a platform together and get them to talk about their perspectives on the world and you will hear, and see, communality. This is exactly what Helen would do. In the manner of the Sufis, who, it is believed, were the first exponents of the Enneagram, she would pass on this knowledge in the oral tradition. Each Sunday evening, in a large hall in Berkeley, she held Enneagram seminars, when she would present the material by interviewing a panel of the same type. The hall was always packed; it seemed that hundreds of people were interested in this take on personality, and how we may "tame" it for our growth. Helen's husband, Chris, was kept hard at work organizing the show, doing the sound, video recordings, taping, and presentation. Helen, up on stage, would create her own magic, interviewing the guests. Afterward, at her home, the panelists and a few invited guests would have a light buffet and talk Enneagram talk. There was something very different about these gatherings. People talked openly about their "passions," the parts of their personalities that they, and others, found challenging. What impressed me most was the level of understanding and tolerance of each other that these guests seemed to have. It was OK for them to be who they were; there was total acceptance and compassion. Was this the answer to misunderstanding in the world?

I began to apply Enneagram theories to my relationships at home and at work with my acupuncture patients, and was amazed at how perfectly they fit. These were ideas that integrated into all areas of my life, illuminating human nature in an unparalleled way.

Upstairs there was a massive fight going on between brother and sister. The mother heard shouting, footsteps thundered downstairs, shaking the walls of the cottage.

"She's done it again," said the son.

"What? What is it now?" asked the mother, somewhat irritated. She'd been down this road many times before.

"She's run out of paper again, she's always borrowing mine, she never gives it back, then I run out and I haven't got any when I need to do my homework."

Mother A *"Stop making such a fuss. It's only a bit of paper, for goodness' sake. Just give her the paper and stop making such a palaver out of it."*

"You always take her side, you never …"

The fight rumbles on for weeks, the argument dredged up from time to time as an example of favoritism and lack of support. Relations between mother and son are strained, to say the least.

Mother B *"That must be annoying! I know how careful you always are to have paper handy, and I bet it's stored neatly, too. But the problem is, I don't have any paper and her project has to be handed in tomorrow morning. Can you do me a favor and lend her some tonight and I'll make sure she replaces it tomorrow and has her own ready in the future?"*

"OK, Mom."

Son goes back upstairs, hands sister the paper and is heard whistling happily in his room.

Before long I was studying the Enneagram in Palo Alto, California, with Helen Palmer and her co-teacher, psychiatrist David Daniels, from the Stanford University Business School, where a class on the Enneagram had for years been the most popular course.

I arrived at my first training week in excruciating pain and on crutches, having broken my foot the day before. With an extra day to get over jet lag, I had gone to Point Reyes to look for elk, and got carried away looking at the seismograph in the visitors' center. Were there really so many tremors all the time in the Bay Area? I walked down a small step and turned my ankle, breaking the heel of my foot and tearing ligaments and tendons. Too proud to ask for help, I limped back to the, fortunately, automatic car and drove through one of San Francisco's famous gridlocks for five hours back to the friend I was staying with. Next day I swung into the course on crutches, not missing the irony. As a type Two this was torment: we are givers, we don't ask for help, we pride ourselves on having no needs. For weeks I had to face my passion every time I needed to open a door. Even at the time, I realized that this was serendipitous, an important part of my own transformation, if not the most essential. Like it or not, I was going to have to look at how pride played out in my life.

Sadly, it took me 18 years to learn that my son was a One, a Perfectionist, and that my first response should be to affirm the time and effort he puts into doing things correctly. Luckily I was given a second chance, an opportunity to build a better relationship. I have the Enneagram to thank for that. I would like to thank him for giving me insight into the integrity and reliability of Ones, and my Seven daughter for reminding me to play. This book is dedicated with love to them; to my valued teachers Helen Palmer and David Daniels; Barbara Turner-Vesselago, who mentored my writing; Fred Lock for teaching me yoga, J. R. Worsley for his unique teachings; Dr. Wang Xin Hua; and Keshe Lama Konchog.

Mary Horsley/Sangye Khandro
October 2004

Mary's highly practical book will help anyone who wants to learn about the Enneagram and teach them to use their body, too. I give it my best and good wishes.

Helen Palmer

introduction and history

When we find the clarity of our true nature,
all the obstacles to happiness fall away,
revealing an inner joy
which, like a flower, is always
ready to respond to the light.

Roy Whenary *The Texture of Being*

An Enneagram is a nine-pointed star (*Ennea* means "nine" and *gram* means "diagram") composed of a triangle and hexagram enclosed within a circle.

The Enneagram is a personality-typing system with roots dating back to the time of the ancient Greek philosopher Pythagoras and to the time of the Sufi mystics. It identifies nine distinct personality types, each with a unique perspective on the world, habit of attention, and presentation.

Once upon a time, walking in the rain forest in southern Laos, I became aware of the clutter I was carrying: camera, binoculars, sunglasses, clothes. I imagined what it would be like to be Early Man, walking naked in the forest. As the fantasy developed, I pictured myself picking up a bright feather to stick in my hair and smearing my cheeks with the red clay of the forest floor. I would build a shelter and decorate its entrance with special stones or interesting bits of wood. . . .

We are all unique individuals, and self-expression is innate, although, at the same time, ironically we have an egotistical tendency to assume that everyone else shares our view. How often do you hear: "Well, she would do that, wouldn't she?" Or: "Everyone feels such and such, don't they?" Well, actually, no, they don't, but crucial to the understanding gained from the Enneagram is that

The nine types

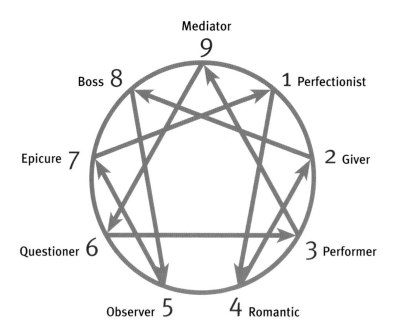

Associated passions

Sloth
9

Lust 8

1 Anger

Gluttony 7

2 Pride

Fear 6

3 Deceit

Avarice 5

4 Envy

Habit of attention

Matching others
9

Looking for what needs control 8

1 Looking for error

Keeping options open 7

2 Serving others' needs

Looking for danger 6

3 Tasks/goals

Avoiding intrusion 5

4 Noticing what is missing

others of the same personality type almost certainly will.

Life is often described as theater. I think it could more accurately be described as pantomime. The average family is more like a battlefield, on which personality is played out, than the cozy tribe advertisements would have us believe. Behavior we find perfectly normal apparently annoys others, much to our consternation. When others rub us the wrong way, we often fail to appreciate where they are coming from. At times life seems to be a mess of misunderstandings.

The Enneagram is a practical tool that shows you how to understand yourself and others better. It identifies nine distinctly different perspectives on the world, nine personality types, which each share a similar point of view. I believe it to be the most effective system I have encountered of human understanding.

The fact is, it is not only material clutter we carry. We arrive on this earth naked, but with an invisible trailer full of baggage. In a study of neonates at Stanford University, in California, it was discovered that after only six months the babies displayed nine distinct ways of relating and that these matched exactly the nine Enneagram types. This confirms my belief: personality is there from day one – something mothers and astrologers have known for centuries. Our parents add a tint through the way they bring us up, the country and place

we are nurtured in add color and flavor, but the basic personality "comes with." And with this "seed personality" we look out on the world and see plenty to confirm our view; we create our own reality.

If we believe the world is a frightening place, there are more than enough terrifying events to confirm it. If we believe we can't trust our caregivers, even the best fail at times. If we believe something is missing from our lives, it will be.

As little children, we develop coping mechanisms, habits of attention, to bolster our fragile personalities, which become inappropriate and no longer serve us well. When we identify our particular viewpoint, and the so-called "passion" that it triggers (see above), immense personal growth becomes possible should we undertake the alchemy of transforming it to its opposite.

Our way of being in the world can restrict us like a straitjacket. The Enneagram, far from being a constraining system, actually provides the means to cast off that jacket and to have more choice in our lives. Although the tendency is to slip back into the comfortable ruts that guide our personalities, and the work will be ongoing throughout our lives, the rewards in terms of improved relationships make it more than worthwhile. Most human beings resist change, and it often takes a major health or spiritual crisis to make us undertake the effort. But it doesn't have to come to that. By increasing our awareness, taking a close look at our habits and the way we live our lives, we can preempt a crisis.

Working for 15 years as a traditional five-element acupuncturist, I constantly saw patients who were ill because of psychological stress; even accidents such as broken bones seemed to occur at times of stress. It wasn't long before I noticed that the form their illness took could be linked to their Enneagram type. What most people do not know is that the acupuncture "meridians" (energy pathways) have a psychological as well as physical function. I saw clear links between the meridians and the Enneagram types. Personality strongly influenced the body, affecting posture and harming organs and functions as well as disturbing the mind and spirit. I sometimes carried out treatments based on a patient's type, supporting the appropriate meridian. When I gave patients "homework" – yoga postures that would free blocks in the particular dysfunctional meridian – they found them very effective. For years I had seen patients make huge strides, reporting psychological as well as physical healing, but this added another dimension.

Until now the influence of Enneagram type on the body has been largely ignored. For example, if we carry fear constantly, it puts an enormous strain on the associated meridians – the bladder and kidneys – creating symptoms such as backache, problems with those organs, and *more* fear. We can reverse the ill effects on the meridians with appropriate yoga postures to stretch and activate them. The positive effect is then fed back and the person feels less fear. The shoulders, often held high and tense, relax, and posture improves; bladder and kidneys strengthen. In Chapters Two and Three I describe postures, meditations, and visualizations aligned to the Enneagram types and devised to heal the emotions and expand the spirit, as well as to heal the body. I also suggest lifestyle changes that support the meridians and ways that you can

How the Enneagram works

The Enneagram is a dynamic system, and although we each have our own primary type, there is also an interaction with four other types. If you are worried about being typecast, remember that the system is more flexible than it might appear. Look again at the illustration on page 8, particularly at the arrows. Each person is strongly influenced by five types:

1   Their primary type.
2   The type they go to (in the direction of the arrow) when they are stressed.
3   The type they go to (against the direction of the arrow) when they are relaxed and happy.
4/5 The types on either side of their primary type, known as the "wings."

The types are further divided into three centers: Eight, Nine, and One are Gut or Anger types. Two, Three, and Four are Heart or Emotional types.

The three centers

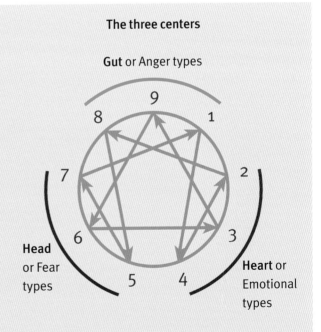

Gut or Anger types

Head or Fear types

Heart or Emotional types

Five, Six, and Seven are Head or Fear types. We tend to experience intuition through the center linked to our type: through gut, heart, or mind.

identify which element may be affected in you. I hope to answer that often-repeated question: "OK, I'm a such-and-such type – what do I do about it?"

Finally, in Chapter Four I introduce you to the most profound level of development possible through the chakra system. Personality has an influence on the chakras, and by describing how type can affect the chakras, and including postures and meditations to balance each, we can take steps to heal this influence.

The history of the Enneagram

The history of the Enneagram is somewhat opaque – and one gets the impression that, as with many esoteric systems, it has been kept deliberately so. Add to that the fact that it has been passed on orally, and much of its history has to be viewed as supposition. It is a vast topic and I am indebted to Eric Salmon for his research. The information I pass on here is largely gleaned from his excellent book, illustrated with cartoons, *The ABC of the Enneagram*.

PYTHAGORAS

There is no ancient carving of an Enneagram symbol, but it is believed that when Pythagoras taught self-development in ancient Greece, showing how to master body, emotions, and mind through silence, asceticism, and discipline, it included use of an Enneagram symbol. It was common then to use geometric figures for teaching, and numbers were believed to hold mystical meaning. It is thought that the Enneagram is the ninth of the "ten seals of Pythagoras" and represents the highest level of development humankind is capable of (the tenth representing God).

Pythagoras taught in the circular Temple of the Muses, surrounded by nine marble statues of the muses, with the veiled statue of Hestia central, guardian of the all-present divine. The muses represented nine universal energies, or facets of human beings, which were symbolically present in the nine numbers.

For many centuries Pythagoras' philosophies were a point of reference: Johannes Kepler in the 17th century used his theory of harmonics to describe the structure of the solar system. Recently it was suggested that the Enneagram symbol may relate to the placement of the planets in the sky, explaining the "hole" in the bottom of the symbol. Since there are no planets visible in the northern sky, I can see that this may well be possible.

THE DESERT FATHERS

In AD 350 Anthony, a wealthy Egyptian, renounced all and went to live alone in the desert, hoping to find himself and understand the Divine – much as Buddha, when a prince, gave up everything to seek enlightenment. Using silence and meditation Anthony endured the harsh conditions and space of the desert to dissolve personality.

Soon hundreds of seekers, all with an interest in inner truth, came to share Anthony's ascetic way of life, each living in solitude. Later, elders took charge of the new seekers and groups formed around "Abbas," or spiritual fathers. The practices of these Desert Fathers closely resembled the Pythagoreans: attention to inner life, analysis of thought and feelings, the fight against the passions, silence and meditation. They believed that a direct connection with God was attainable.

EVAGRIUS PONTICUS (345–399)

Significantly for the Enneagram, among these Desert Fathers was an educated Greek theologian, who was the first to write down his ideas. He soon became prominent and defined a symbol much like the Enneagram as we know it, and eight evil or distracting thoughts – later to become the seven deadly sins. Evagrius also recorded information about the dynamics between types:

> *I first need to recognize my type in order to be able to attract my vice … I have to observe where my energy glows, what blocks me, and what blinds me. The source of my greatest weakness is also the source of my most important gift. Through my passion, I can discover my main talent, and then my passion will be transformed and I will be able to enable the divine fruit that I have inside of me to flower.*

One of his texts mentions nine paths of distraction: anger, pride, the search for glory or vanity, sadness, envy, avarice, gluttony, lust, and sloth. It seems that we are getting close to the Enneagram as we know it today.

SUFISM

Two centuries later, in the same area that spawned the Desert Fathers, Sufism, the mystical tradition of Islam, was born. *Jihad*, as they understood it, meant the holy war against the ego. The Sufis followed the same principles as the Pythagoreans – self-knowledge and observation, being in the present moment, allowing each action to be guided by God, harmony with the universe, physical and artistic pursuits, symbolism of numbers, and meditation. However, the Sufis used the diagram and theory of passions in a way that was different from the Christian view on sin and passion. The Enneagram at that time connected the Christians and the Sufi culture, and the two religions, so distanced from each other today, once intermingled most creatively.

DANTE AND CHAUCER (14TH CENTURY)

Dante in the *Divine Comedy* and Chaucer in the *Canterbury Tales* address the transforming of the passions. In the *Divine Comedy* nine ways are suggested as to how they may transform their passion to reach heaven, by not choosing the easy way and falling to the nine circles of hell. Chaucer relates each sin to a corresponding virtue, gluttony to sobriety, avarice to compassion, just like modern Enneagram teaching.

GURDJIEFF (1877–1949)

Gurdjieff could be called the father of the modern Enneagram. Born in Alexandropol, on the Black Sea, George Ivanovich Gurdjieff experienced many different religions and cultures. He traveled far and wide, and it is from Asia Minor that he claims to have brought back the Enneagram. A larger-than-life figure, mystic, and spiritual teacher of immense personal magnetism, Gurdjieff used the Enneagram, calling it a "Sufi oral teaching device," to bring about transformation in his followers. Tales abound of him encouraging his dinner guests to drink huge quantities of alcohol and then confronting them with their chief feature. He did not define the nine types as such, however, but if he intuited that fear was the chief feature of one of his guests, for instance, he would make them meditate alone in a graveyard at midnight.

Gurdjieff also used movement, like the Sufis, to experience the Enneagram. Students were ranged around a circle at nine stations, and performed careful movements in patterns that indicated the dynamic between points, sometimes following the path of the arrows inside the circle from 1-4-2-8-5-7. This was an experiential way of learning the Enneagram, and occasionally produced profound reactions in his students.

The Orthodox Church and the Tibetan tradition also influenced Gurdjieff. I recognize his methods, urging people to engage the inner observer, to meditate and identify their passion, from my studies and practice of Tibetan Buddhism.

OSCAR ICHAZO (1931)

The son of a high-ranking Bolivian civil servant, Ichazo also traveled for many years in the Middle East. He claims to have learned about the Enneagram from Sufi teachers in Pamir, Afghanistan, who taught him their secrets before he became acquainted with Gurdjieff's writing. Ichazo taught at the Institute of Applied Psychology of Santiago, Chile. In 1970 he led an 11-month spiritual-development course in Arica, Chile, which included 50 key people in spiritual development from around the world, including Claudio Naranjo and Alexandro Jodorowski. It was Ichazo who linked the nine passions to the Enneagram diagram and was the first in the West to teach the Enneagram in this way.

CLAUDIO NARANJO (1932)

A Chilean doctor and honorary faculty member, teaching at Harvard and Berkeley universities, Naranjo learned the Enneagram from Ichazo. His research linked the passions, Gurdjieff's work, with modern pathologies, and identified the major defense mechanisms underlying the types. He developed the method of teaching the Enneagram by interviewing panels of the same type.

HELEN PALMER (1937)

A teacher of psychology and intuition, Helen Palmer learned about the Enneagram from Claudio Naranjo in 1971. Among others, this class of '71 contained Cathleen

Speeth, Hamina Lee "Amas" (who spoke fluent Arabic), and Bob Ochs, a Jesuit priest. Helen Palmer has written two international best sellers on the Enneagram, including *The Enneagram, Understanding Yourself and Others in Your Life*. She is co-director of the Trifold School of Enneagram Studies with David Daniels.

DAVID DANIELS, M.D. (1934)

Clinical professor at the Department of Psychiatry and Behavioral Sciences at Stanford Medical School, in California, David is co-founder of the Trifold School of Enneagram Studies. He taught the highly popular Enneagram and Leadership course at Stanford Graduate School of Business with Michael Ray.

Author of *The Essential Enneagram*, David devised the professional training program with Helen Palmer, and together they have taught hundreds of professionals around the world since 1988.

BOB OCHS

A Jesuit priest, Ochs was one of Naranjo's students in 1971. A teacher at Loyola University, in Chicago, he taught the Enneagram to a class of 12 graduate priests who have since taken it all around the world.

The first Enneagram book

Written by three students of Bob Ochs – Father O'Leary, Maria Beesing, and Robert Nogoseck – the first Enneagram book was published in 1984. Thus, the Enneagram passed into the public domain, much to the disapproval of those who thought it could be dangerous to popularize such a powerful system of personal transformation.

The Enneagram today

Many people have put their own particular stamp on the Enneagram, and it seems that it has been thus since the times of Pythagoras. What is clear is that it is a powerful tool for transformation and that people from all around the world acknowledge it as such. I have met teachers from Finland to South Africa, from China to the USA; it is truly global nowadays. The Enneagram is used in the business world, in missions, churches, and schools for personal and spiritual development. Nearly every person whose sleeve is touched by the Enneagram finds that it resonates in some way, often transforming their lives.

Why study the Enneagram?

Benefits that expand and unfold over time:

Understanding yourself To learn why you react positively to some people and negatively to others. As you grow in understanding you will become more conscious of your natural strengths and be able to recognize and dissolve what prevents you from working with or relating to others.

Pinpointing and managing stress The Enneagram helps you identify where 90 percent of your stress comes from, and teaches methods, some very ancient, to reduce it. For the first time this now includes yoga postures, as well as meditations, visualizations, simple practices, and practical lifestyle changes to harmonize your life.

Understanding relationships You will gain a better understanding of the dynamics of past and present relationships and the role you played/play in them.

Reading people and serving clients The more you learn to understand your friends, relations, clients, and lovers the better you will be able to respond to their needs, clearly express yours, and build lasting relationships.

Communicating and working with others Gaining deeper insight into yourself and others enhances your ability to work more effectively with your loved ones, work associates, and friends.

Each type has its struggles. No type is better than any other – we are, if you like, all perfectly flawed. No type goes better with any one particular type than another: awareness is the key. I recommend that you read this book with an open mind and compassion in your heart. It occurred to me recently that there are no grown-ups; each one of us is merely a child of the universe, from movie star, president, or preacher to street person. All of our futures depend on our ability to get along with each other and make the best job of it we can. As the Dalai Lama says, "My religion is kindness." What better way to practice this than by understanding ourselves and each other better. I hope you enjoy the journey as much as I.

CHAPTER ONE

The nine types

In the silent emptiness of our true being, there is also a fullness and completeness . . . there is nothing that can provide us with greater happiness, because we are already in bliss.

Roy Whenary *The Texture of Being*

introduction to the nine types

Nine guests, each representing a type, are sitting around a circular table: there is a gap at one end, giving an unrestricted view of each one (see diagram opposite). Pay close attention, for you are about to meet the characters that people your world.

Type Nine, the Mediator

At the head of the table sits the Nine, eagerly anticipating the opportunity to make a good connection with someone at the party. Distracted by a book, however, she ended up throwing on the first dress that came to hand. At the moment she is trying to make peace between her two neighbors, who are disagreeing about a movie.

Type One, the Perfectionist

He spent a long time preparing, trying on and rejecting several ties before he could find the perfect match, and he is still worried he hasn't got it quite right. He is exasperated with the man opposite, who won't accept that the movie is historically incorrect and unethical.

Type Two, the Giver

She spent hours preparing food to please all her different guests, and bought two new outfits in an attempt to get her image just right. She is flirting outrageously with the man on her left, who might just be able to give her a break in his new company.

Type Three, the Performer

He almost forgot to come to the party because he was so busy, but is enthusiastically describing his new company, and frantically networking. He has already left the table twice to answer calls on his cell phone.

Type Four, the Romantic

She was depressed before she came out, and almost canceled. She's in a deep red, velvet dress with a unique brooch pinning her wrap. She is silently toying with her food. Something is missing, but she can't quite put her finger on it …

Type Five, the Observer

He didn't want to come because, for a start, it would interrupt his research and, additionally, because he hates social events. Soberly dressed, he was ready in minutes. He sits silent and withdrawn, watching the others, near the door so he can make a quick escape.

Type Six, the Questioner

A crack in the ceiling right above her head has caught her attention and she is wondering if the roof will fall in. She was suspicious of the shellfish hors d'oeuvres and worries that she may have left the iron on at home.

Type Seven, the Epicure

If that conversation about the movie doesn't lighten up soon, he's thinking he'll go to the other party sooner rather than later. Or he might catch that late film … but since three desserts have just arrived, he'll sample each of them first.

Type Eight, the Boss

He creates most of the noise at the table. Clearly enjoying every minute of the argument with the One, he is slapping the table to make his point, pouring more wine for everyone, winking at the hostess opposite, and squeezing the knee of the Nine.

Finding your type

Somewhere in this scene is your partner in personality – but don't worry if it is not immediately obvious which one was most like you, because more detailed descriptions follow. It is also quite normal to have the "oh, shit" experience (am I really like that?) rather than the "ah ha" experience when you discover your type.

Higher mind states and virtues

Our true nature, our "higher mind state," is clear, perfect, joyous, and light – identifying the obstacles to finding it is one way to find happiness. When you work with the Enneagram to recognize and transform your passions, the higher mind states and virtues (see right) are more likely to be experienced.

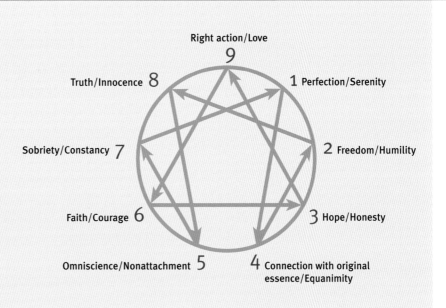

Right action/Love
9
Truth/Innocence 8
1 Perfection/Serenity
Sobriety/Constancy 7
2 Freedom/Humility
Faith/Courage 6
3 Hope/Honesty
Omniscience/Nonattachment 5
4 Connection with original essence/Equanimity

Sometimes it helps to find your type to remember how you used to be when you were least conscious – say, around 18 years of age.

Editing the hard disk

Sadly, we all have a tendency either to edit out or focus to an inordinate degree on the more positive or the more negative sides of our personality. But unless we acknowledge all aspects of our nature, we can never hope to be fully rounded human beings. Just like a computer, the disk is in there, helping to run the machine. Helen Keller, the deaf and blind woman and role model to millions, said that if you keep your face to the sunshine, you cannot see the shadow. And if you think about it, it is the shadows that give us depth. The more difficult side is actually your teacher, and should be welcomed as such.

Heart and stress points

As I said in the general introduction, at different times in life you may be more or less influenced by the wings (the types that lie on either side of your own) or by the heart and stress points (see the diagram on page 8). The type you will mimic in times of stress is the one that lies in

the direction of the arrow. You can use the way you respond to stress, or when you are particularly happy, to help to confirm your Enneagram type.

The triads

Another clue is to figure out which triad you are in (see the diagram on page 10). If fear is your issue, start by checking out the fear types: Five, Six, and Seven. If image is all-important, look at Two, Three, and Four. If anger is your issue, look at Eight, Nine, and One.

Finally

Try to resist judgment about the other types. Remember that they, too, have equal lists of good and bad points. Rather, use the descriptions to help you appreciate the qualities of each type.

This is not necessarily an easy thing to do, and most of us need constantly to remind ourselves, when our personality trips us up, that it is a lifework. But the rewards come surprisingly soon, and we feel *good in our skin*, as the French say. The aim is to make the likelihood of attaining the higher mind state and the virtue specific to each of the types more possible.

type one the perfectionist

ANGER

God is in the details.

Ludwig Mies van Der Rohe

The world would be a sorry place without the Perfectionist Ones. While the rest of us are muddling by on "good enough" the Ones are putting in the extra hours, dotting the i's and crossing the t's. If you want an event organized scrupulously, down to the smallest detail, ask a One. You won't need to check on their progress: you can trust that all is already covered. Take a vacation with a One and it will be organized like a military campaign: schedules checked, packing completed several weeks in advance, hotels booked, itinerary planned to the nth degree. Oh, and the Swiss Army knife packed and checked in, not carelessly left in carry-on.

When we go on vacation my wife always leaves backward and on her knees. She cleans the whole house, top to bottom just before we go, finishing with the front door step. If we need a last minute pee, there's no way she'll let us back in – the boys and I have to use the flower bed around the back of the house.

I know a One who has her Christmas presents bought, wrapped, and stowed away in the attic by the end of September every year. She never forgets a birthday or fails to send a thank you note whenever she has come to dinner – however casual the arrangement. This point is very important: for Ones it is paramount to act correctly and to be seen to act correctly at all times. They are people who can be relied on to act with complete integrity. It is a black-and-white

world for the One. They have a sense of the right way to do things, and if we err from that path they are likely to tell us. Elton John said of playing with Ray Charles that he was meticulous about his own performance and about his (Elton John's), too.

I was driving to work when I saw a mother on a scooter with her son riding behind her, no helmet on; he must have been 9 or 10 years old. I was incensed. I caught up with them at the traffic lights and told her exactly what I thought about her endangering her child's life like that.

The One's home is spotless, ordered, and tidy, as is personal appearance. Shoes will be polished, tie straight, and shirt matching if it is a man; if a woman, nail polish will be unchipped and handbag coordinated. The other morning I heard Carol Thatcher on the radio speaking about her mother, Margaret, a former British prime minister. She described how important it was to her mother to be formally dressed at all times, never to be caught looking un–prime ministerial. She boasted she needed only a few hours' sleep each night; Ones are highly energetic people.

To say Ones are organized barely touches on it. There will always be a spare toilet paper roll in the bathroom and coffee in the cupboard. Should the scissors be needed, the One will know exactly where to find them, and they will be sharp. If the elastic in your underwear goes, barely has it snapped before a One will produce a safety pin from their bag.

My friend came around and we spent the evening trying on clothes. When she left I had to re-iron every single garment, even though most of them were probably fine. It was a Monday night, I had to go to work at 7 the next morning, and I didn't get to bed until 1 o'clock.

Ones are idealistic, honest, fair, incredibly self-disciplined, and ethical; they make good editors and journalists since their prime habit of attention is to notice mistakes. They are often to be found working for charities, in environmental organizations, or in politics. Nelson Mandela, a probable example, earned the respect of the entire world for his dignity and perseverance in detention and for achieving the miracle of transforming his country without a bloodbath.

All this does not come without cost. Whereas most of us are aware of our inner critic (or negative inner voice) beating us up at times, Ones report that theirs never lets up. It is a constant background voice, nagging them day and night, telling them that they "could do better." It's an exhausting way to be, and can prevent them from feeling fulfilled even when they've done really well. As children they felt painfully criticized and learned to monitor themselves minutely. We should feel great compassion for the One, whose striving for perfection can seem endless and wearing – a definite downer on the fun side of life. Pleasure is permitted only when all the tasks are done.

I tell myself that I can go for a walk when I've washed the car, fixed the fence, marked all the essays, cleaned up the house, and sorted out my file index system. Of course, by the time I've finished that lot, I'm exhausted, and somehow I never do get to take that walk.

Anger – the passion for a One

This habit of attention, looking for fault, rarely ends with the One. The downside of valuing perfection above all else is that the rest of us inevitably appear flawed. We often disappoint Ones, who expect others to strive for perfection equally. They can suffer from a "hardening of the oughteries."

Believing that they have to be perfect to be loved, it is particularly hard for the One to accept criticism, and it is easier to project fault onto other people (the mind-set identified as "judging mind" in Buddhism). They may nurse a grudge about the unfairness of trying so hard and yet not having their efforts fully appreciated.

Sometimes it feels hard to please the One, and cope with the inflexibility: we may end up feeling controlled when Ones insist on things being done their way. They are often extremely dedicated and efficient parents, but their children may need reassurance that mistakes don't mean they are not loved. Although parents only partially shape our personality (as I said before, I believe we arrive with our own "map"), Ones often themselves describe having a demanding type One parent. They tell of longing to feel appreciated for their efforts. A key to getting along with a One is to own your own mistakes – they, above all people, will understand how you feel. Offer a sincere apology and confess. You will be amazed at how it opens their hearts.

In relationships jealousy can be an issue:

When I left him our mutual friends had nothing to do with me. For years I could not understand why such close friends had dropped me like a stone. Then one day I found out; he had insisted they do so.

If Ones fail to identify the anger that underlies their habit of attention, it can affect their close relationships. One of the problems is that Ones see anger as a "bad" emotion. It tends to get locked into the body as a knot of boiling rage. It helps Ones enormously if, when they do access their anger, you stand your ground and hear them out. It also helps Ones to do something physical: running, digging, squash, yoga, and so on. There needs to be an outlet for the building resentments, release from the endless worrying.

There's something about running. . . . I'm out there pounding along, breathing from the belly, I suppose. It puts me in a place of such serenity.

Life can become overly serious for the One through procrastination of pleasure. I am always glad when I hear of so-called "trapdoor" Ones who, in situations where they are away from home, let down their hair. I was thrilled when Monica, from the comedy series *Friends*, who epitomizes type One, landed in bed with Chandler for a night of hot sex on an outing. She is an endearingly drawn character, and if ever a One feels that they are unlovable I highly recommend they watch a few episodes of *Friends*; pay close attention to the pivotal role of Monica.

So how does a One find release from their habit of attention of looking for fault? "Good enough" is not sufficient – and yet, ironically, this is their release, the key to growth and finding serenity. For a One, the task is to leave the white thread on the dark blue carpet and notice that the world does not end. Ones find peace when they develop the inner observer, who sees when the inner critic is being tyrannical, and by taking a moment to count to ten, breathe, and observe what is going on in the body. When areas of tension are identified, they can be released. Ones are "body" types; when something is not right they feel it in their guts. This is their intuitive center. It helps to check in here and identify appropriate effort.

The wonderful thing is that, largely by simple mindfulness, the inner critic can be disarmed. You can even put a dunce's hat or a dog's nose on it and make it look ridiculous! I have observed great serenity in Ones who have become mindful of their habit, quieted the critic, and allowed a higher consciousness to be heard.

Type One – the dynamic movement of energy

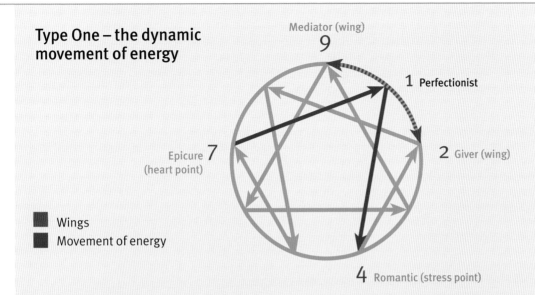

Mediator (wing)
9

1 Perfectionist

Epicure 7
(heart point)

2 Giver (wing)

4 Romantic (stress point)

■ Wings
■ Movement of energy

The wings

As I said in the introduction, the wings have an influence on type (see pages 16–17). A general rule is that an emphasis on the previous wing, counterclockwise around the circle, is more beneficial.

A type One with a strong Nine wing is a bit more chilled out, and is more able to be detached. It helps a One to slip into Nine mode, to become distracted from doing right, to relax and become "at one" with the situation rather than correcting it.

Type Ones with a stronger Two wing are often warmer and more helpful, but may be more controlling and critical.

The movement of energy for a One

As you can see from the diagram above, the forward direction of the arrow leads the One to type Four on the Enneagram symbol – the Romantic. This is where Ones go when they are under stress, becoming more emotional. Rather than focusing on a sense of loss and isolation when they find themselves in this space, it helps the One to spend time in creative, artistic pursuits. I suggest that pottery might be a particularly therapeutic way to deal with the negative feelings. In the process of making a pot you have to knead and bang the clay hard for several minutes to rid it of air bubbles (great for pent-up anger), followed by a quiet softness and connection with the clay as you mold and shape it. Flaws in the glaze or in the form can by grace transform an ordinary pot into something quite beautiful . . . alchemy created both by and in the One.

When a One is feeling relaxed and happy the energy moves to point Seven, the Epicure. This is the true place of transformation, where their guard may be let down. How lucky the One is that their path to serenity is in play. To see a One when they are in this space is truly a divine sight. I picture Nelson Mandela dancing, his whole being radiating pleasure, at one with the universe.

How Ones can nurture themselves and grow

• Meditate regularly and notice when the anger comes up, and the effect it has on your body.

• Develop a habit of leaving things less than perfect, and notice that the world does not end as a result.

• Learn to recognize appropriate energy to put into a task.

• Stop, breathe, listen, and hear when someone praises you.

• Exercise in enjoyable ways, such as dancing, running, walking, sex – whatever you find fun.

• Practice yoga regularly and make sure that you include in your routine the posture for Ones on pages 108–9.

• Write a letter to your inner critic, thanking it for past advice that was appropriate, and then send it firmly packing. Burn the letter.

• Put a ridiculous nose/hat on your inner critic when it is nagging you.

• Allow yourself to lose your temper.

• Root out your "shoulds" and "oughts" as ruthlessly as you would de-junk your closets about the house.

• Spoil yourself – flowers, chocolates, meals out – and regularly indulge in the things that you enjoy .

• Practice leaving the thread on the carpet, the cushions un-fluffed, papers scattered.

• Wear odd socks occasionally just to see how few people notice, or care if they do.

• Welcome impulses and desires, and see them as valid.

• Tell yourself that you are perfect just the way you are.

• Notice when you slip into the repeating habit of resentment, and work toward transforming it into serenity.

How we can support a One

- Show appreciation for the extra effort they put in to making sure things are right.
- Take them out to play.
- Remember that when they criticize us, they are a thousand times harder on themselves.
- When you are glad of their advice, say so.
- Be fair with them.
- If you are wrong, say so and apologize.
- If a One does access their anger and express it openly, stand your ground and listen.
- Provide an ear for their worries.
- Even if they are happy to take on all the responsibility, do your fair share.
- Affirm that you love them just the way they are.

"What I like about being a One"

- The ability to cover a lot of ground because of good administration/organizational skills.
- Liberating to know (now) that my way is one of nine ways of being, and that trying to be perfect is a no-win strategy.
- The instinctive sense of direction that brings order from chaos.

"What I dislike/find difficult about being a One"

- The pressure on myself to try to be perfect makes me anxious and tense.
- It is very difficult to stop working (finding things to do that to my eyes need doing).
- Lack of confidence that what I do, say, think is the "correct" thing to do, say, think.
- Comparing myself endlessly with others to my own detriment in family and work settings: "she is a better mother than I am"; "he is a more effective boss than I am."
- It is very hard to hear feedback clearly because I am always listening for criticism.

"How you can help me"

- Give me feedback very carefully and, above all, constructively, so that I can hear what you are actually saying.
- Help me to play/slow down and laugh at myself.
- Acknowledge how hard I try/how much effort I expend.

type two the giver

PRIDE

I'd like to be a queen in people's hearts.

Diana, Princess of Wales

Twos at their best

Empathetic

Warm

Supportive

Appropriately
generous

Intuitive

Adaptable

Loving

Loyal

Selfless

Enthusiastic

Twos at their worst

Manipulative

Smothering

Gushing

Possessive

Give to get

Indirect

Hysterical

Superior/Aloof

Seductive

Resentful

Passion

Pride

Repeating habit

Flattery

Higher mind

Freedom

Virtue

Humility

Diana, in one simple sentence, more or less sums up the mind-set of the Twos. Twos arrive in this world with one agenda – to be helpful and so earn love. Believing they are not inherently lovable for themselves, but that they have to earn it with giving, they fear rejection. A huge amount of effort, often to the point of exhaustion, is put out to meet other people's needs. Sometimes called the Helper, this type notices what to give to gain approval.

The Two develops fine-tuned radar for other people's needs from a very early age. If love is not forthcoming they may try a little charm. Pop out the thumb and say, "I like your pretty necklace!" or "Are you thirsty, Mommy? Can I get you a drink?" They were Mother's little helper, Daddy's right-hand man.

I used to lie awake waiting for Santa to come, but when my mother tiptoed through the door to lay the stocking on my bed I pretended to be asleep, because I didn't want to spoil the surprise for her in the morning.

Unbelievably stretched at work? Here is the Two with a cup of coffee. And probably it will be just how you like it, accompanied by your favorite cookie, and an offer to help you sift through all those e-mails. They will remember your birthday and send you a carefully chosen card, and if you go through a personal crisis, expect them to be on the doorstep. Pretty soon you may be wondering

how you ever did without them. Twos make loyal friends and supportive partners, they are not usually leaders, and they are more comfortable being the power behind the throne, for they gain prestige by reflected glory. But watch out for the sting: did I hear, "You didn't get where you are today …"? Twos abound in the caring professions as nurses, doctors, and health workers, and in the social services and service industries. They work as personal assistants and personal shopping guides (remember Rachel in the sitcom *Friends*?). They make friends easily, and often keep them for years.

Her funeral was absolutely packed. I looked around at everyone's faces, at their grief, and realized that like me, every single one felt she was their special friend. We were a crowd of "best" friends.

Of course everyone is different. In order to be liked by such a wide variety of people it is necessary for the Two to be a little flexible. A little editing may take place. Why tell Robert, a pro golfer, that you can't stand golf and find it the most boring game on the planet, when you can get into a conversation about the pleasures of a good walk across the course to the ninth hole? After all, he's drop-dead gorgeous and if you were honest about your dislike he might reject you.

I should have been suspicious when he suggested "that place" for our honeymoon, during rainy

September. Trudging around sewage farms in the dead of winter with a pair of binoculars around my neck looking for great crested grebes was bad enough; what had I been thinking of, agreeing to a honeymoon during the autumn migration? It sort of set the tone for a marriage that was doomed to fail.

Diana, Princess of Wales, like her friend Mother Teresa, epitomized the Two. Charitable, hardworking, devoted, maternal. Twos make the perfect host/hostess, happy to pass the hors d'oeuvres, or to introduce you to the person who would be just right for your company or for you to employ as nanny to your children. Twos are cheerful, friendly, generous, warm, and energetic: these are the fuzzy puppy dogs of the Enneagram. They are "happy to be of service." Or are they?

Pride – the passion for a Two

The Two works hard at relationships. This is their territory – they are Heart types who intuit feelings quite literally in their hearts. The passion is pride. They pride themselves that they know just what your needs are and only they can fulfill them. This you might find very seductive if you are in a relationship with a Two. And that is not the only way they can be seductive – they may be fuzzy puppy dogs, but these are fuzzy puppy dogs in a thong.

When I went to a party I'd notice who was the alpha female and I'd think, "I'll have that one." I would lay on all the charm, figure out what she liked to talk about, whom she'd like me to be. As I hooked her, I could literally feel pride swelling in my heart because she had chosen me to go home with.

Twos also report changing tack midway through a sentence when they intuit that their opinion is not going down well. But where in all this adapting is the Two? Who is he/she? In all this giving and adapting to meet others' needs, somehow their own get lost. They are so repressed that their own needs become very hard for a Two to recognize. And guess what? You are supposed to intuit them. Unenlightened. Twos also pride themselves that, unlike the rest of the world, they don't have needs.

So avoidant are they of appearing needy, that if you have hurt them you may never know it; they are past masters at putting on a brave face.

I spent hours cooking him a dinner that I knew he would like. I put a lot of effort into the table arrangement and I even bought a new dress. When he came, half an hour late, with an apology that he already had a commitment, I heard myself saying with a smile, "No problem, that's fine, call when you're free...." I crumpled into tears the minute I closed the door behind him.

At some stage in your relationship with a Two you may begin to feel a little bit uncomfortable about all this giving. The cheerful friendliness may feel more like gushing, over-the-top Pollyanna-ism. Twos may not be Jewish, but they do an excellent impression of the Jewish mother archetype. The scales may feel too heavily weighted in your direction. You try to give, but somehow more always comes back. It can feel impossible not to feel indebted.

A patient brought me five goldfish in a bucket, and told me it had taken him almost as many hours to catch them for me. I hadn't asked for the goldfish (I had frogs in my pond and I knew the fish would eat the spawn) or for him to spend five hours catching them for me, and coming to my house to deliver them on my day off.

Type Two – the dynamic movement of energy

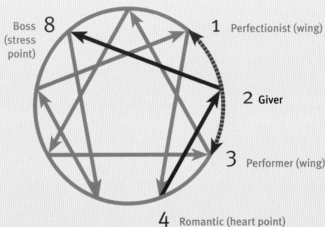

8 Boss (stress point)
1 Perfectionist (wing)
2 Giver
3 Performer (wing)
4 Romantic (heart point)

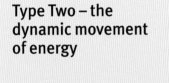
Wings
Movement of energy

The wings

Twos with a stronger One wing will be more judgmental, and more self-critical. However, they will also be more objective and have strong ideals. The regularity of the One mode is supportive to the Two, and can help to cool down rising hysteria when needs are not met.

Twos with a strong Three wing really shine as party hosts, and will be more ambitious and concerned with being the center of attention. It is often said, "If only Twos could do for themselves what they do for others." Using their Three wing can help Twos claim their own power.

The movement of energy for a Two

When Twos are stressed – for example, when their subconscious needs are not met – they move to point Eight, the boss, whose chief feature is vengeance and the need to control and be assertive. Let's go back to the phrases "they are happy to be of service" and

Twos have a habit of flattery. You wanted to go out for dinner on your own with your partner for your birthday … how come she's laying on this big thing with lots of people? Was it by any chance that conversation about your erudition, how witty you are and your fabulous dress sense that seduced you into accepting the invitation? It helps Twos when they can hear themselves going into this mode.

Twos report it is very important when they begin to become aware of their repressed needs, and to verbalize them, that they be heard and acted on. It can feel monumental to ask for help. If they are heard and the request is acted on as if completely normal it frees Twos to continue to state their needs honestly, rather than manipulating a situation to have them met. The whole relationship is cleaner, healthier, and more balanced. By the by, there is a myth in Enneagram circles that Twos do not like to receive – far from it, they just need a little practice and encouragement. The Two also needs to learn how to accept gifts/help graciously and simply, without going over the top.

Humility deflates pride. An evolved Two gives cleanly without expectation of a return and can perform acts of generosity quietly and discreetly without any need of a fanfare. They are humble enough to recognize that they do have needs and that like the rest of the world they are interdependent. This is the path to the higher mind for a Two: freedom.

"they are loyal and supportive friends" and add a caveat – as long as you intuit their hidden agenda and needs.

For many years I was personal assistant to a company CEO. I can't remember what triggered it – maybe he'd been paying more attention to his other assistant or something – but I had to get my revenge. I took him his morning coffee and put a couple of really delicious chocolates on a saucer on the tray. He was on a diet, and I knew he wouldn't be able to resist them.

Now the Eights may snort and say, "Call that vengeance?" For a Two, however, who wants to be seen as nice and helpful all the time, this is the type of subtle vengeance you can expect. But it could be the vengeance that drops poison in the wineglass rather than stabbing with a knife! Remember the way Princess Diana posed alone in front of the Taj Mahal?

On the plus side, it can help a Two to verbalize their needs when they go toward the Eight, to find the energy to stick up for themselves and to fight.

When a Two is feeling loved and at peace, the movement of energy is toward the Four, the Romantic. Unfortunately this can mean that when happy in a new relationship there may be an insecurity that emerges: "This is so beautiful it can't possibly be real," "It may not last," "It could end in tears." On the plus side, it is in Four that the Two may access their creativity, with a potential for enormous spiritual growth. They are better able to spend time alone appreciating nature, music, art, drama, and so on.

I realized I had never been alone before for a substantial period of time. One day I decided to crack this unhealthy need to be constantly around other people. I told all my friends I was going away for a week, took the phone off the hook, and stayed at home alone. By the end of a week reading, writing, walking, gardening, meditating, and doing yoga I wondered how I had ever managed without time alone. With no one to distract me, I became aware of my own needs, how I liked to structure my days. Nowadays I regularly take time alone; it brings me great peace – a sense of freedom.

How Twos can nurture themselves and grow

- Spend time alone, at home, walking, in nature. Take a vacation alone.
- Notice when anger arises and look to see what need you are repressing.
- Give a gift to someone anonymously.
- Learn to recognize the swelling of pride.
- Notice when you are being flattering.
- Meditate regularly and notice when the mind wanders to other people, and gently bring it home.
- Practice yoga regularly and pay particular attention to the posture for the Twos on pages 110–11.
- Observe yourself changing opinion/style/hobbies to match another person.
- Remind yourself that not everyone likes you, and that this is normal.
- Practice telling the truth honestly without a positive spin, even if it is negative.
- Remember how good it makes you feel to help someone? Give others the chance to enjoy that feeling.
- Practice saying no, and don't give a long explanation.
- Learn to recognize not only flattery, but also pride so that you can work toward changing it. Invite in the transformation to its opposite – humility.

How we can support a Two

- When they express a need, respond to it.
- Let the Two know they are loved for who they are, not for what they give.
- Be generous to them, tell them it makes you feel good, and they will learn to receive.
- Encourage them to take a break, relax, and do nothing, while you cover. Share fun times with them.
- Soften the blow when you criticize; they are very sensitive to it.
- Remember their birthdays.
- Encourage their creativity.
- If they are special to you, or important, let them know it.
- Don't be disheartened when they want to spend time alone. Encourage it.
- Ask to hear their problems and don't let them focus just on yours.

"What I like about being a Two"

- I find it easy to make a connection with all kinds of people in different circumstances.
- I have lots of interesting friends.
- Generosity is second nature.
- It is easy to empathize with others and intuit their needs.
- I have loads of energy and enthusiasm.

"What I dislike/find difficult about being a Two"

- I am regularly exhausted trying to serve everyone else's needs.
- I often forget to honor my own needs.
- It's almost impossible to say no.
- I tend to give negative feedback to people.

"How you can help me"

- Make me sit down and take a break occasionally.
- Welcome the times when I present myself in a less-than-positive light.
- Show me that you appreciate me when I haven't done anything for you.
- Help me learn to ask directly for help, rather than dropping hints.

type three the performer

DECEIT

"I'm not flying, I'm falling with style."
Buzz Lightyear

Struggling to get your project off the ground? Interest flagging in your business? Need to turn it around? Better find a Three. Decisive, risk-taking, adaptable, optimistic – no type equals the Three in terms of energy and motivation. We are talking speed, drive, enthusiasm, and visibility. They expect success and, more often than not, they get it. The multi-tasking Threes are unlikely to be involved in just a single project – adept at keeping all the balls in the air, they are frustrated by the fact that the computer can't keep up with them, no matter how often they upgrade.

Optimism is positively stellar. Hang around with a Three and pretty soon you, too, might be persuaded that you could buy that Porsche you lust after, and that money does indeed grow on trees. Worrying is for wimps. Threes are highly competitive – winners. Entertainer Joan Rivers describes being competitive from third grade, and pop icon Madonna achieved her ambition to be the most famous woman in the world. The F word in their case is Failure, and it is not in their vocabulary. Their horse is going to come in first; you'd be a fool not to back it. Look at the odds! A cautionary note though – don't turn up with your empty pockets pulled out asking for an explanation of why his horse finished second to last. If the Three notices you standing there looking all forlorn (unlikely because the Threes don't really do forlorn), he will convince you that the horse was merely saving his strength for the race on

Saturday. "Bound to win next time. Besides, Saturday is the big one. . . ."

Life is to be lived to the max: Threes are the human doings of the Enneagram. Up at 5:30 A.M., check e-mail, take a run, cell phone calls to various people on the way to work, lipstick at the traffic lights, a call to the nanny to make sure she remembers daughter's dentist appointment, and to daughter to tell her to have a nice day at school, and be sure to ace the test. Cell phones, laptops, PDAs – all the gizmos of the modern world were probably invented with Threes in mind. They are high achievers and they expect their families to be up there on the ladder with them.

I came in from school with the result of my math exam. I thought 98 percent was pretty good, but all she wanted to know was what went wrong. I made a pact with myself to get 100 percent next time. After that I got straight As all through high school and at university.

Breakfast is on the run or networking at the Rotary; lunch is a meeting (with a few calls during). The appointment book is full and the secretary had better be a wonder at dealing with double bookings. Evenings are rarely spent relaxing (why waste all that time?). If they are not working, then they are down at the gym honing the body beautiful.

Type Threes are supermoms, company directors, politicians, prime ministers, presidents, head teachers, the movers and

shakers of this world. They may even be therapists, as long as they are the best-known therapist in the district. They proliferate in the building profession, but not balancing buckets of cement on their shoulders. Oh no, they are the architects, the owners, building up an empire along with your house. Image is all-important to a type Three. Hollywood is positively awash in Threes, all trying to outperform each other on the red carpet with the flashbulbs popping, not to mention in films; lifting, tucking, filling, and padding their bodies to perfection. They are often successful athletes and sportsmen and women. Wherever it is possible to have a high profile of success, look for the Threes: they are definitely not going to be collecting your garbage.

Look – failure is not an option. I'm not going to start a project unless I think I can succeed with it, or turn it around if it's

failing. If I do feel that it's flagging, I don't hang around long enough for it to bother me – I'm on to the next thing. And in my own mind I tell myself that it was pretty successful anyway and no big deal. If they hadn't let me down with the equipment deliveries, the project would have flown. But mostly I'm just not thinking about it.

Generally known as nice guys, generous people, they are often handsome men or attractive women with infectious, winning smiles. It is easy to be inspired by their success. More often than not, you just can't help liking them and enjoying the glow of their backslapping bonhomie. They are the Buzz Lightyears, ready to save the world, thriving on praise, enjoying being seen as one of the guys.

Which brings me back to the issue of image. A Three would never be caught out in the wrong gear, be it power suit, white coat, or wet suit and flippers. They would rather change their image several times a day than be seen not looking the part. Listen as the prime minister Tony Blair changes his accent when he is speaking to different groups of people. He sounds different addressing members of Parliament than when he is speaking to shop-floor workers or rock stars. And he is known for loving the "dress-down" style, unlike Thatcher, when he thinks it'll make him one of the guys.

Threes are highly prized in American society, which is often referred to as a "Three culture." President John F. Kennedy (who hid a severe illness) was most likely a Three. Threes are less valued in England and in other parts of Europe, but Britain nevertheless has Tony Blair and France has Jacques Chirac. In Hollywood we find Tom Cruise, Sharon Stone, Arnold Schwarzenegger, and Nicole Kidman among others. David and Victoria Beckham are good examples, as is Mick Jagger.

Deceit – the passion for a Three

I wonder if you felt the lift in energy as you read the description of the Three. Maybe you are even becoming a little exhausted, wondering how these guys survive. You may already be sensing the problem for the Three in this strong identification with the task, with the product: deceit for the Three lies in this identification.

If you believe you are loved just for your achievements or image (which is changeable), might this not feel a little hollow at times? What if all you want deep down is to be loved for yourself, not for what you have achieved? You may be able to convince the adoring masses that you are what you do, but can you go on deceiving yourself?

The thing is, when the task is done I feel good only for a moment. It's a high literally for a second and then it doesn't have any juice, so I have to keep moving on. I'm never done. I've never really felt that I've achieved anything.

How does the little Three child feel when he sees other little boys and girls, who are regularly bottom of the class, getting a hug from their moms anyway? When you are rewarded only for high achievement, and believe that therein lies love, what happens when you fail? What happens when you can no longer keep on top of the emerging wrinkles? If, when you stop and are quiet, the illusion shatters, how does that feel? Self-esteem for a Three is actually very tenuous; it's like a hungry monster impossible to satisfy. Threes are Heart types; that is their intuitive center. It is often their hearts that pay the cost – look at Tony Blair. Human doings are also human beings – a body can take only so much.

I daren't stop. If I stop and relax, all I can feel is this great hollow space inside, and I don't like the feeling … so I get up and fix something or start another project, or go out for a run – anything rather than face that empty place where feelings come up. I can deceive myself that I don't have them, that everything is fine, as long as I'm busy. Anyway, if she knew the real me, she'd leave, wouldn't she?

If we are intimate with a Three we may find it difficult to keep up with them. In the early stages of wining and dining, you may be deceived into thinking that this is how it will be forever. But watch out. If the spotlight is removed, the Threes are gone – moved on to the next project before the glue has dried on the current one. And winning your love might just have been a project.

What of the husband or wife of a Three who wants to curl up on the sofa and occasionally veg out on movies? Or who tires of "adventure" vacations and isn't that keen on the Three's latest fad sport? You've got the fabulous car, the kids are well educated, and you live in a great neighborhood – what more do you want? It may fool them that this is what they want, but does it fool you? Tears and emoting are hard for the Three to take. Uncomfortable with their own feelings, yours may become burdensome, distracting them from their task. Trophy husbands and wives aren't expected to complain. Don't get me wrong, Threes put enormous energy into making a relationship work (not wanting to be seen to fail). It's just that "doing" may not hit the spot if "being" is required. It may not feel authentic to their partners.

Type Three – the dynamic movement of energy

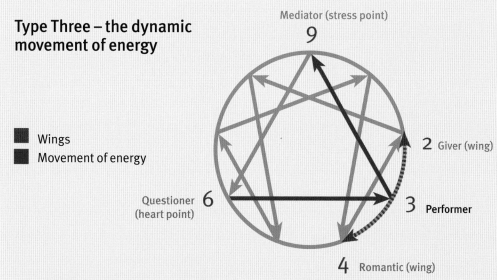

Wings
Movement of energy

The wings

Threes with a strong Two wing are better able to listen to others' needs, are more compassionate, warmer, popular, sociable, more seductive, and better able to acknowledge their feelings. They are also more likely to find time for relationships.

Threes with a more developed Four wing are more creative, artistic, and imaginative, and may be more emotional, introspective, and pretentious.

The movement of energy for a Three

When Threes feel secure, the energy moves to type Six, the Questioner, or Loyalist. They find it easier to spend time with friends, can pay more attention to the needs of a group rather than controlling the agenda, and can allow themselves to explore their feelings. However, they are also more vulnerable in this space and may experience the doubting mind and fear of a Six.

When I finally managed to feel secure, I started to doubt myself. It was a strange feeling, not at all pleasant. In a way, life was easier before I started to question it – but at least I am having feelings.

In stress, type Threes go to the Nine space, the Mediator. They report that overworking can cause them to crash into complete inactivity, virtually to the point of catatonia. Sadly, it is often not until the first heart attack has occurred that a Three will stop and take stock.

Details are burdensome to the type Three personality. What happens when the corners that have been cut to get the job in hand done finally catch up with them? You thought the building was sound – why did the roof fall in? Is the Three going to be around to face the consequences? If you keep on taking up the baton of the next task because things are getting a little sticky with the current one, how great is your achievement really going to feel?

Our passions are not comfortable, but they truly are our friends, pointers to how we may transform. When the Three can pay attention to how they deceive themselves and others, and the illusions are dissolved, the path to honesty opens. The higher mind of a Three knows hope – on a deep level, the hope that trusts that everything is unfolding as it should and is guided by a higher power. When they learn to pass authority over to this higher power, it helps them really feel satisfaction.

How Threes can nurture themselves and grow

- Try taking a backseat at a meeting and listening to others.
- Take a day with the family, doing whatever they choose.
- Take time every day to meditate. Pay attention when feelings arise. Instead of pushing them down, practice staying with them and observing the effect on the body.
- Notice when the urge to leap up and go arises in meditation. . . . Sit for at least another five minutes and gradually increase this time.
- Schedule regular long, slow baths scented with relaxing oils and surrounded by candles. Take a book with you, or maybe even your partner.
- Look at where you are now in terms of success, and learn to appreciate that.
- Next time you go on vacation, leave the laptop behind, and all matters relating to work. Try to choose a better balance of adventure and relaxation.
- Start your day by writing in a journal for 10 minutes. Put down whatever comes into your mind – just freefall. When feelings arise, record them.
- Book a weekly massage.
- Unlock the tension in your body with daily yoga, and do the posture for Threes shown on pages 112–13.
- Practice meditating on impermanence; it will help you determine what is important.
- Identify deceit in your behavior, and vanity, to invite in the opposite – honesty.

How we can support a Three

- Praise them for who they are, not for what they do.
- Encourage them to take time out and chill.
- Don't overburden them with your feelings.
- Remind them that nobody says on their deathbed: "I wish I'd spent more time at the office."
- Create peaceful and harmonious surroundings.
- Threes are Heart types, so take them to a weepy movie and give them plenty of warmth.
- Don't fuss around them when they are working.
- Remember they have low self-esteem at core, so appreciate their projects and give them honest feedback gently.
- Tell them that you love them just the way they are.
- Get them to slow down and look at the dew on a leaf or a spider making a web.

"What I like about being a Three"

- My "always on" energy.
- The certainty that if I take something on it will be successfully completed.
- My sense of achievement.
- Receiving other people's recognition and praise.
- Optimism – there will always be a way to sort out the problems. Hey, problems are opportunities!

"What I dislike/find difficult about being a Three"

- Stopping and smelling the roses.
- Relaxing.
- Finding time for contemplation and self-reflection.
- The pressure to achieve.
- Other people's perception that Threes are shallow or don't care.

"How you can help me"

- Encourage me to make a "task" of relaxing – for example, scheduling in yoga or meditation time.
- Praise me/say you love me when I haven't done anything.
- Notice and encourage my emotional responses.
- Notice and draw it to my attention when I'm producing status-driven responses.
- Encourage me to do one thing at a time, with my full attention.

type four the romantic

ENVY

My soul is a broken field, ploughed by pain.

Sara Teasdale

Fours at their best

Artistic
Empathetic
Creative
Outgoing
Warm
Supportive
Helpful
Compassionate
Intuitive
Expressive

Fours at their worst

Over-dramatic
Self-absorbed
Moody
Depressed
Guilt ridden
Intractable
Withdrawn
Moralizing
Shame ridden
Rejecting

Passion
Envy

Repeating habit
Melancholy

Higher mind
Connection with
original essence

Virtue
Equanimity

You weave dreamily along the shore, leaving footprints behind you that fill with golden water. Feeling the sand scrunching between your toes, you remember when you walked here arm in arm with your lover. Was it really only yesterday you parted? The reddening clouds seem more intense today, the fragrance of the flower sweeter. You can still taste the hint of salt on his lips as you kissed good-bye. A fairy tern swoops low, her trailing tail feathers brushing the water. You wish you were that bird, so carefree, so graceful. Your heart lifts a little and you draw your wrap around you, the breeze like cool satin ribbons on your skin. "If only … if only," you sigh.

Welcome to the territory of the Four.

I was anxious about the passenger sitting on my right. She had wept continuously since we left San Francisco, and we were two hours into the flight. I touched her arm lightly. She removed her headphones. "Are you OK? Is there anything I can do?" "No, thanks," she sobbed, "it's just this music, it's so, so moving. . . ."

We are talking sweet yearning, poignancy, and intensity. These are the romantics of the Enneagram, artists and creators, people with feelings on an off-the-scale level. The opposite of aesthetic is anesthetic. And if there are two things sure to anesthetize the Fours, they would be "boring" and "ordinary."

The Four child felt abandoned. There was a perfect love, but it was withdrawn; it might happen again. The loss might be literal, as when a parent leaves or dies, or it may be an inherent sense. Either way the attention is the same. It focuses on loss and abandonment, on what is missing.

Look in any area of life where creative people gather to find Fours. They are acting in films, on TV, on stage, painting, and writing, playing, or composing music. Famous Fours might include Oscar Wilde, Sylvia Plath, Keats, Shelley, Anais Nin, Bette Davis, Prince Charles, Vincent van Gogh, Rudolf Nureyev, Martha Graham, Virginia Woolf, Edith Piaf, Joan Baez, and Marlon Brando. When Fours are therapists they are involved in deep and transformative work. If they are chefs they are creating unique dishes; if interior decorators they are furnishing houses with flair, using subtle and unusual colors. A Four is capable of transforming a scene with a single white lily. Candles illuminate their bathrooms; their bedrooms are heady with the scent of exotic oils.

Yesterday I was digging when my attention was drawn by a shard of bright blue glass glinting in the sun. I straightened my back and marveled at the shard managing to stand out in all that brown soil.

Fours are like that. Even when they sneak in at the back, they somehow make an entrance. There is a kind of sweep of the cloak (men or women) even when they are not wearing one. They love their unique

style, and unlike the two other Heart types, the Twos and the Threes, they would not dream of changing it to seek your approval. If you want to woo a Four, give them a carefully chosen and unique present – it will make them feel special. It doesn't have to be expensive. (I once gave a Four the empty egg case of a grass snake that I found on my compost heap – she was thrilled.) Ordinary life is seen as mundane by Fours. Clashing colors, chairs made of plastic, inelegant fabrics, offend their taste.

Fours enjoy their rich emotional life and take pleasure in creative melancholy. They deal with the sense of loss/ abandonment in three distinct ways. First, some may be deeply depressed, as distinct from melancholic. This they find does not serve them creatively, but freezes them in a world of introspection. Second, other Fours do not appear depressed at all. In their search for the perfect mate, job, or whatever, they may appear positively

hyperactive, always on the move from one affair to another; they are "up" the majority of the time. The third type of Four swings wildly between the two.

People ask me, "Are her emotions all over the place now that she's pregnant?" I say I haven't noticed a difference!

Since we all live in an aesthetically challenged world, this habit of attention can become a problem for the Four. The much-yearned-for love, the fabulous goddess that they have created in their minds, who alone can make them feel complete, is as likely as the rest of us to have spinach stuck to her tooth. Disappointed, they leave, and suddenly the unobtainable takes on a rosy hue. They remember her tiny hands, the touch of her lips, and long to be once more in her arms. Enfolding her in an embrace they notice that she's put on a little weight since they were last together. Thus continues the push-pull pattern that is common to Fours in their search for the ideal. As soon as Fours get what they want, be it man, woman, job, or cottage with the roses around the door, attention shifts to what is missing. How could it breed anything but a sense of disappointment?

Ironically it feels more satisfying for Fours to yearn for the unobtainable than to actually have it and risk losing the emotional intensity. The girl on the aircraft was not actually distressed in the sense that would be understood by other Enneagram types. They like to amp up the emotions; it makes them feel alive. But there is a conundrum here. Because there is a certain amount of pleasure involved in the melancholy, they can actually snap out of it quite easily:

Her ex was there, flirting with another woman. She slunk into corners, gazed longingly at him from the shadows, and shared her intense pain with anyone who came near. It was beginning to sour the party. In the end I said, "Just buck up, will you, I've got a party to run here and we need your help. I haven't got time for all this drama." She gave a little smile, picked up the hors d'oeuvres tray, and sashayed into the crowd.

This brings me to the empathic part of their nature. When you are going through difficult times, Fours are most generous in their support. They do not shrink from the challenging areas of life: birth, death, breakdown. Fours live there. It has to be said that Fours can even be reckless in their pursuit of intensity, and need to pay attention when this happens. They describe suicide as an option.

Envy – the passion for a Four

Feelings of loss are internalized into a sense of personal lack. No matter how much they succeed the Four tends toward feelings of unworthiness, shame, and self-hatred.

Whenever I go to a party I look around and I see what other people are wearing, and I always notice people wearing fabulous outfits or wonderful accessories, better than mine, that I would like. It makes me feel inadequate, ashamed.

We see a successful, creative person; they see failure and lack. They see others with the perfect partner, job, home, and so on and yearn to have the same. This habit of mind can make them extremely competitive – but there is a catch. Have you ever had the experience of reaching the top of the mountain, only to find that there is another peak farther ahead that you hadn't known was there? The longed-for goal once attained disappoints, fails to fill the empty hole. The sights are set once again on the far peak, in a wave of longing.

Transformation is possible when Fours can shift attention to what they have rather than what is missing. When we place our attention always on the past or on the future, rather than in the present moment, it is enormously sapping of the vital spirit. It is a fact that wherever we put our attention, energy follows, far healthier than to keep it in the present moment. Focusing on what we lack, especially through a distorted lens, will deplete anyone, but particularly the Four.

Fours need to note it whenever they feel themselves slipping into feelings of loss. They should bring the attention into the present with the breath, and run through a checklist of what they do have, of blessings – be it good health, loving partner, or beautiful home. I recommend that Fours open a gratitude diary. Start and end each day by writing down five things for which they are grateful. It may sound simplistic, but I highly recommend it to anyone going through a tough time, not only Fours. It saved me during a very dark time in my life. At first you may find it difficult, but as time goes on this exercise works its magic, shifting the focus in a deeply transformative way. At the very least it starts and ends the day on a positive note. When Fours can make this change they regain a sense of deep connectedness with the universe, and of their own original essence or god-like nature.

Type Four – the dynamic movement of energy

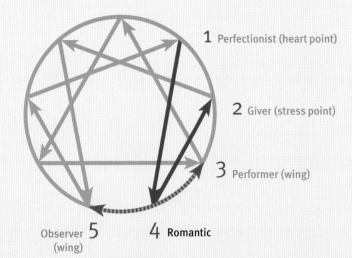

1 Perfectionist (heart point)

2 Giver (stress point)

3 Performer (wing)

Observer 5 (wing)

4 Romantic

■ Wings
■ Movement of energy

The wings

A Four with a stronger Three wing is likely to be more ambitious, flamboyant, and extroverted (running a unique business, for example). Less likely to be mired in self-inflicted shame, they are better able to move into action, and feel less sorry for themselves.

With a stronger Five wing, the Four is more introspective, is more likely to have a solitary, creative life as a writer, artist, psychologist, therapist, or something similar. However, they may be more depressed.

The movement of energy for a Four

When a Four is feeling good, the energy shifts to One, the Perfectionist. Attention to detail can bring them into the present, to be more self-disciplined and less buffeted by their emotions. The perfection of nature brings them great equanimity, the higher mind for a Four. However, they may be more critical and angry with us for not understanding them, moralistic, and more personally disappointed.

In stress, the Four will tend to move toward Two behavior, and can repress their own needs. A Four "in Two" may compound the belief that a perfect partner will be the answer to all their problems. They may somatize their distress, becoming ill to gain attention. On the plus side, they are more empathic, less self-absorbed, and make better connections with others.

How Fours can nurture themselves and grow

- Bring attention into the present time.
- Notice what you have instead of what is missing.
- Update a gratitude diary first thing every morning and last thing every night.
- Notice when you are "amping up" your emotions, and take the breath to the belly center and focus there.
- Practice yoga regularly, paying particular attention to the arms and the chest. Perform the posture for Fours illustrated on pages 114–15.
- When you find yourself moving into reckless mode, ground yourself by doing something such as gardening or running.
- Perform a loving act toward yourself every day.
- Make a structure for the day and let it provide a steady rhythm for you.
- Work on reining in your emotions when they threaten to overwhelm you.
- Know that when you envy qualities in another, these are your own unacknowledged qualities.
- Set time aside to mourn your losses with music, rituals, and attention, then let them go.
- Remember that all things pass.
- Notice your habit of envy so that you can choose to transform it to its opposite – equanimity.

How we can support a Four

- Remind them of their good qualities and what we find special and appreciate about them.
- Help them to live a structured life.
- Give them carefully chosen, unique presents.
- Take time with them to enjoy artistic pursuits.
- Remind them of their accomplishments.
- Don't dismiss their depression and moodiness, but help them with creative diversions.
- Let them have time alone when they need it, but encourage them to socialize when it's appropriate.
- Tell them that you appreciate their artistic sensibilities and ask their advice.
- Take them for walks when they can connect with the earth and be surrounded by nature.
- When you are inspired by them, let them know.

"What I like about being a Four"

- Being able to relish what is beautiful on every level – sensual, emotional, intellectual.
- It makes my life enjoyable and rich.
- The intensity I can feel in being alive.
- Being able to go through "dark" times – especially grief or sadness – knowing that I always come out of it at the other end.
- A sense of how my life could be even better – it keeps me working at it, and keeps my life getting better and better.

"What I dislike/find difficult about being a Four"

- Feeling poor even when I know I'm not.
- A need to be important and respected.
- Not really expecting people to include me.
- Wishing I just had lots of upbeat, happy friendships.
- Constantly comparing myself with others, my attention noticing "out there" what others seem to get out of life.
- Always being afraid that you will leave me.

"How you can help me"

- Don't allow me to manipulate you. Be grounded and stay true to yourself and tell me what is going on for you. That inspires me and helps me out of my drama.
- Allow my feelings, understanding them if you can, even if you don't agree.
- Doing things together. If I'm depressed, invite me to join in some sort of physical activity, preferably one that is fun, to break the spell.
- If we disagree or fight, let me know that we are still connected and that we are in this together.

type five the observer

AVARICE

Less is more.

As we move into the private world of the Five I would like to invite you on a brief inner journey. As you sit or lie reading this book, imagine your body contracting, in a containment of your energy. Blend with your environment; try not to stand out. No sudden movements, poking out elbows or knees, quiet and still. Now picture yourself at a desk, surrounded by informative books. The desk has neat piles of current books, for research you are doing, and behind you and all around are shelves filled with books and files. The phone is set not to ring and disturb you. The computer screen flickers to one side. You are in a small office at the end of the garden, with a gravel path to forewarn you if anyone approaches.

Your house is furnished minimally, and your wardrobe has an adequate amount of clothes in fairly neutral colors, and no more. There is little ornamentation, but what there is, is carefully chosen and has a particular significance. The house has a neat, academic air. Hours pass; the day has an ordered, predictable rhythm that you find comforting. Then you hear the gravel scrunching on the path. Your wife/husband is approaching with a mug of tea. This is irritating because it disturbs your train of thought, and it is all you can do to grunt when you take it. Relieved, you watch them disappear back up the path to the house.

My wife knows now when I'm doing it. I have a word for it. I tell her "I'm Fiving" and she knows to leave me alone.

At this point I could ask you how you feel – but that might mislead you. Feelings are a disturbance to Fives, likely to upset their containment. The Five child felt intruded on. Their perception of the world is of it butting in on their thoughts – the thoughts that they enjoy ruminating on so much. They may have had scant space to call their own as a child, or it could have been more mental intrusion, with what seemed like exhausting requests for emotional engagement. The survival strategy of stinginess with time they allow others evolved to protect them from this: they withdrew, both physically and emotionally. A tip: it is better to allow Fives to approach us than to pursue them.

Fives live in the predictable world of thinking. Often intellectual, they are happiest in their minds. Emotions tend to be secreted away to deal with at a later time and, meanwhile, they replace them with thinking. Ask a Five what they feel about something and they will often say: "I'll let you know. I need to think about that." And don't be surprised if you have to wait a week or two for the answer. I once asked a Five what happens when they fall in love – surely a huge and uncontainable emotion.

I think that sexual/one-to-one attraction falls outside the definition of feelings for a Five, or for this Five at any rate. Physical attraction can cause a leap inside (such as when I meet my wife after a separation). Fives are good at touching in a one-to-one situation because they

are not distracted by having to say something and it avoids the need for words. Other feelings and the search for the right words are not necessary and do not intrude into showing tenderness and love for that one person, so Fives are usually very good at the physical side of relationships. All the repressed feelings can be represented this way.

Fives make a tremendous sacrifice when they allow someone into their castle. Nobody ever gets close in normal circumstances, so a commitment to allow someone in is an immense step for them to take and that person must seem to be extremely worthwhile to be worthy of the sacrifice.

I have never thought about this before, but my feeling of love does not seem to be suppressed like other feelings, and I wonder if Fives choose which feelings to suppress, however subconsciously. I've never discussed this with other Fives and I think that would be difficult since they will usually not admit to having feelings or even recognize that they have them.

It is not my experience that Fives are unemotional people – they can be very warm and loving – it is just that there are limits to how much this emotion is expressed and when. They enjoy anticipating events in detail, but in the moment there is disconnection from their feelings.

When an Observer is present, they prefer to be left alone. The temptation might be to try to draw them out at your dinner parties. Don't! It is very stressful for Fives to be put under the spotlight. They will speak in their own good time, and probably with great erudition, but just don't force it or you may find that they disappear quietly. Whereas a Two or a Three is energized by company, the Five is drained.

Uninvited guests should be careful not to overstay their welcome … because it is a brief one.

I shared this quote with another Five, who added:

No, uninvited guests are not welcome!

You have been warned. Fives are happy working alone at home, in the cloistered environment of a study at a university, or in a research lab. It hardly needs stating that they are not great ones for socializing and prefer to stay in at home.

Let's go out … your place or mine?

The American artist Edward Hopper was renowned for his reclusive nature, and David Mean, in Alan Yentob's excellent BBC documentary, said that he was the first painter to capture the essence of souls that were alone. Famously, he drew a line on the floor of the studio that he shared with his (Two) wife, barring her from crossing it while they worked. His response to her histrionics was to leave cruel cartoons about their fights on her desk.

Have you noticed that, in the main, the Five quotes are very concise? Fives are not people inclined to waste energy on a lot of unnecessary words. They get to the point slowly and precisely, and would like the rest of us to do the same. Hopper was once asked to give a speech. It consisted of a single word: "Thanks." If you need an in-depth conversation with a Five it helps if you book an appointment in advance, agree on a time limit for it (preferably not more than 10 to 15 minutes), and stick to it.

Fives avoid strong feelings, yours or theirs, and, because they are one of the three Fear types of the Enneagram, they especially avoid fear. Each Fear type has a distinct way of dealing with this emotion. The Five internalizes the fear. Fearful of being proved foolish, they avoid feelings of inadequacy and emptiness by hoarding knowledge, and are thus comforted that they will always know more than the rest of us. Before any action is taken, the topic will have been fully researched in private. So it is not that the Fives are inactive – it just might look like that to the rest of us. In truth, their minds are constantly busy.

Fives compartmentalize their thoughts. A topic is dealt with exclusively at any one time and then neatly filed away. No wonder our interruptions are so disturbing to them. Unlike the multi-tasking Threes, the Fives are only comfortable dealing with one thing at a time. They are at home in academe, which allows them the private time to do this without a boss on their back (they resist authoritative control) and are often scholarly, erudite people. Albert Einstein was probably a Five as well as J. D. Salinger, J. Paul Getty, Emily Dickinson, Jeremy Irons, Meryl Streep, Buddha, and Franz Kafka. A good film to watch to get a sense of typical Five behavior is *The Remains of the Day*. Watch Anthony Hopkins in the role of the butler.

Avarice – the passion for a Five

The problem for the Five, running such a tight control on their emotions, is that to the rest of us this can seem cold and unemotional. Unlike Twos, who repress their emotions, the Five is detached from them. If you confront a Five with a problem that is affecting you emotionally, sometimes a considered reply in a week may not cut it! It begins to feel like a very unequal exchange and the Five can appear distant, stingy with their emotions – another way they manifest avarice. Their habit of withholding can isolate the Five, and make the people around them feel rejected, unwelcome. Some Fives suffer terrible loneliness as a result.

The need to know more for fear of being found wanting sometimes results in the Five appearing arrogant. Albert Einstein said that only two things are infinite: the universe and human stupidity. And he was not sure about the universe.

The avarice can extend into all areas. John Paul Getty installed a phone booth in his hall for visitors to use. He was also loath to enjoy the personal comfort his money could have bought him, preferring to stand in the rain waiting for a lift from a friend, rather than fritter money away on catching a taxi.

As with the other Enneagram types, identifying how the passion – in this case avarice – operates in our lives is the key to release. When a Five can identify avarice as it

Type Five – the dynamic movement of energy

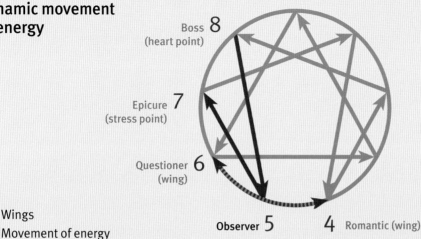

■ Wings
■ Movement of energy

The wings

Fives with a stronger tilt toward the Four wing are more able to get in touch with their emotions, are likely to have a more creative flair, and are more empathic. They may, however, also be more self-absorbed.

With a stronger Six wing the Five is more fearful, but also more loyal. Their analytical skills may be more pronounced, and they may, for example, be scientists.

The movement of energy for a Five

When a Five feels secure, the energy tends to move against the direction of the arrow to point Eight. Here, they can access more energy and that, in turn, helps them to get into action. They become more in touch with their bodies and are able to be more outgoing and outspoken. Instead of withdrawing from an angry exchange they are better able to express it. On the other hand they may be less reasonable, openly ignoring other people's feelings.

A Five in stress moves toward the Seven, the Epicure, which, although it feels quite uncomfortable for them as they become more scattered and distracted, is actually quite a beneficial place for them to visit. The playful side of a Seven helps the Five to lighten up and move out of their castle, to experience more diversity in life and to release some of their inhibitions.

arises, then they have a choice – and as I have said before, the Enneagram is all about choice – to work on the areas in their lives that cause them, and the people around them, difficulty, or stick with the difficulty. When Fives can observe themselves going into "withhold" mode, they can choose to change it. When outer observer is transformed into inner observer, transformation is possible, and being observers by nature they should have a head start on the rest of us.

They tell me that meditation is comparatively easy for them – lucky Fives. It helps a Five to become more physically active, to stretch the boundaries of their bodies by moving their limbs. Yoga is a science, with much depth on all levels, and I find that Fives really enjoy it. You can do it in a group, but practice alone at the same time – an ideal way for Fives to dip their toes into the social arena, be intellectually stimulated, yet remain assured that they won't be intruded on.

How Fives can nurture themselves and grow

- Get in touch with your body by taking up a sport.
- Do the yoga exercise on pages 116–17, especially first thing in the morning, to energize the body.
- Give yourself a frivolous, luxury present every now and again.
- Find a place to talk about feelings, such as psychotherapy. Preferably in a group.
- Write down your dreams as you wake, particularly noting feelings you had in the dream.
- Buy a watch that beeps the hours and so bring your mind into the present each time it does so.
- Go walking with your family or with friends instead of going alone.
- Notice when you are trying to impress people with your knowledge.
- As soon as the inclination to give to others arises, obey your first (usually more) generous instinct.
- When the urge to withdraw comes when someone is emoting, stand your ground and drop your breathing to your belly.
- Notice avarice when it arises so that you can choose to change it, and transform it to nonattachment.

How we can support a Five

- Give them plenty of space and privacy.
- Allow them time to answer your questions without interruption.
- Don't demand too much of their time and energy by being clingy.
- Be patient asking a Five to express their feelings; allow them time to go away and think about them first.
- Don't gush around them. A gentle welcome will suffice.
- Enjoy quiet pursuits with them rather than big parties, rock concerts, or a mass gathering of relatives.
- If you need to unburden to a Five partner, be brief and choose an appropriate time.
- Allow them to approach you, rather than you them.
- Do not try to draw them out on social occasions.

"What I like about being a Five"

- I like to stand on the edge of a group and not get involved and always have a withdrawal route planned.
- I like becoming so absorbed in a book that I hear or notice nothing else going on around me.
- I like the solitude of being completely alone.

"What I dislike/find difficult about being a Five"

- I sometimes find the sense of intrusion when in a group to be absolutely overpowering.
- I always try to sit on the edge of a group or near a door so that I can make a quick, unobtrusive exit if necessary.

"How you can help me"

- Appreciate that I need time alone to sort things out.
- Respect my privacy at the times I do not need company.
- Realize that I am not trying to cut out anyone or withdraw from anyone in particular – just company in general.
- Gently, ever so gently, explore the feelings that are buried deeply within me.

type six the questioner

DOUBT

No passion so effectually robs the mind of all its powers of acting and reasoning as fear.

Edmund Burke

Hush! What was that noise? You thought you were alone. You check behind you. Did you remember to lock the door? Heart pounding, shoulders tense, but unaware of this, you hear only the deafening silence as you scan for danger. Who is it? What do they want? How can you escape? The door pushes open slowly. The cat pads into the room and you scream: "Don't do that! You startled me!"

I don't know about you, but my heart is also pounding, even though I intentionally wrote myself into that scene. Alfred Hitchcock, past master of the genre, said that there isn't any terror in a bang, only in the anticipation of it. But what if the terror does not end with the bang? Can you imagine a world that is one long terror, full of doubts, mistrust, and shaken confidence?

I tremble and shake. There is something about being in the limelight. I have to figure out if people are well disposed toward me or not. I'm always scanning, watching out for sudden movements, listening to the tone of voice – for who is a friend and who is not.

Born of this habit of scanning for danger, Sixes have a talent for noticing what might go wrong, be dangerous. They are particularly good at noticing hidden or implied dangers. Take a Six with you when you look around a house you are thinking of buying. They will notice the rising damp, leaking taps, broken light fittings, and smell the blocked drains, while you are still in raptures over the fabulous views.

My husband, a Three, was having trouble in his company. Something was going on that was sabotaging the business, but he couldn't quite put his finger on it. I went in, purportedly to sort out the filing system, and quietly took in the scene. It didn't take me long to detect what the trouble was; it was like electricity in the air. There were two people in the team who absolutely hated one another.

Sixes thrive in professions where this habit of attention can be put to good use, and where their mental powers are valued. They can be found in all areas of life, but are commonly found working in the legal profession, the police force, the business world, the armed forces, and academia. Sixes work well in groups. Famous people who demonstrate typical Six behavior are John McEnroe, Paul Newman, Woody Allen, Robert Redford, Julia Roberts, Hamlet, Krishnamurti, the Reverend Jim Jones, and Sherlock Holmes.

This is an energetic type: time seems to have no meaning to the Six as they clock up the overtime, totally engaged in what they are doing. (Just don't slam the filing cabinet shut behind them.) They are practical,

---

Sixes at their best
Compassionate
Warm
Dutiful
Reliable
Hardworking
Practical
Caring
Witty
Likable
Loyal

Sixes at their worst
Paranoid
Controlling
Defensive
Tetchy
Unpredictable
Judgmental
Rigid
Sarcastic
Rebellious
Insecure

Passion
Doubt

Repeating habit
Cowardice

Higher mind
Faith

Virtue
Courage

helpful, responsible, and dutiful. Sixes have a particular affinity for supporting the underdog, are compassionate, and are often to be found working in charities. A word of caution, though: there is an innate distrust of authority that goes along with the Six terrain. Bosses will have to earn their trust, and while there is doubt, the Six can become secretive and rebellious. If you work for a Six, or they for you, make sure you are scrupulously honest, consistent, and reliable.

They are sometimes called the Loyalist, and when you have won the trust of a Six you will find them warm, reliable, loving, faithful, and supportive. I especially value their highly developed quick-witted sense of humor, which brings great benefit to the family or work team. There is probably no better example of the fine wit and the anxieties of a Six than Woody Allen. Watch almost any of the films he appears in to study the type.

Also watch the sitcom *Friends* and pay particular attention to Chandler. (The others in the series jokingly complained that he always got the best lines.) He once introduced himself as the one who makes jokes when he feels uncomfortable. It's easy to confuse the anxiety of a Six with that of a One. Watch *Friends* and note the different ways in which Monica and Chandler are anxious. Monica is more concerned that she and everyone else get it right (in her terms). Chandler is more generally anxious. Angry Sixes express it with wit, sarcasm, and biting remarks. Commonly there are accusations and a defensive lashing out when a Six feels threatened. This is fear projected onto other people, which is the Six way of dealing with it.

Sixes are adaptable much as Twos are, but the difference is in the expectation, the lack of trust at the end of the exchange.

There is less need for connection and approval; it's more a question of getting along with someone to diffuse any threat, but without great involvement. My needs are met with the immediacy of the safe connection – but I don't anticipate that it will last.

The Six child saw the world as a dangerous place full of threats – and, as I stress again and again throughout this book, whatever your habit of attention, there is plenty out there in the world to confirm your view. They often report not being able to trust the adults who cared for them, and developed a doubting mind. You can see it in the eyes of a Six: when they are not scanning right and left looking for danger they are often wide open, like a startled rabbit caught in the headlights.

Be careful how you praise a Six. They won't believe you unless you are a very close and trusted friend. Their tendency is to think, "What do they want?"

Every week I would pick flowers from the garden to put on my desk at work. I had plenty of flowers in my garden and always picked extra for reception and for my colleague's desk. It took me a while to figure out why she looked so suspicious when I did this – she thought I wanted something.

Here is an important point to consider if you think you are a Six: they have two distinct modes. The counterphobic Six, as opposed to the phobic Six, may not look like a Six at all, and may be given to skydiving or bungee-jumping off a cliff in an effort to prove to themselves and to the world that they are not afraid. They may be working in the business world and looking very strong, talking to huge audiences – they may even be the leader of a great nation – but they are still basically afraid. With their defensive mode, counterphobic Sixes in particular can often be mistaken for an Eight (the Boss) as well as the Performer Three (their stress point).

Doubt – the passion for a Six

Intuition is a wonderful thing, and Sixes experience it in abundance, but problems arise when fears are imagined and turn into paranoia. How do you differentiate between a reliable insight and one that is born out of irrational fear?

I had just parked my car in town, and was going to leave it there for the morning. As I was getting my bags out of the back there was something about the person walking past. . . . I just knew he was going to steal the car radio. It was as if there was a flashing neon sign saying, "I'm going to steal your radio." I locked the car and walked on slowly. He ducked into a post office. I went into a store pretending to be shopping. He saw me and turned around and went away. He didn't steal the radio because I'd put him under surveillance.

Maybe – but maybe not. Sixes report that they can suffer meltdown – an upsurge of worry and doubt. It wells up and they feel taken over. I describe more about fear in the next chapter on the Five Elements, but it is of note here that there is a connection between the ears and fear. Have you ever experienced trying to reassure someone who is terrified and they seem to go deaf on you? If you are supporting a Six gripped by fear you will need to meet them halfway and be honest and very patient – they have well-developed bullshit monitors.

Don't tell me that the worst won't happen. I can show you plenty of evidence in the papers that it does. Let me know that you understand that the worst could happen, then remind me that I have dealt with whatever it was before and survived.

Survival in this frightening world for the Sixes (the Questioners) lies in their ability to recognize their passion, in this case a doubting mind (they are also known as devil's advocates), to be able to identify when they are running the worst possible scenario (WPS), and to work back from there. Being a Head type, checking out the facts with a trusted friend or family member is one way of dealing with the amplified fears. The task for the Six is to develop faith to counter the doubt – quietly to count to ten, follow the breath in and out at the belly, and calmly see things for the way they really are. (There are instructions for meditation in each of the following chapters.)

Type Six – the dynamic movement of energy

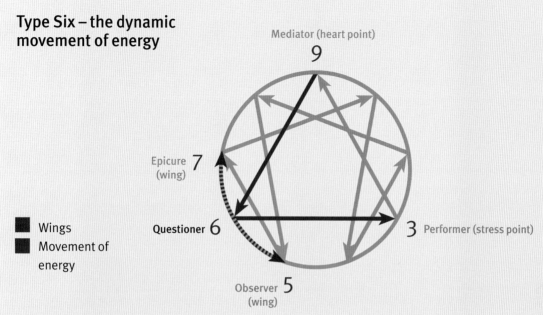

Mediator (heart point)
9

Epicure 7
(wing)

Questioner 6

3 Performer (stress point)

Observer 5
(wing)

■ Wings
■ Movement of energy

The wings

Sixes with a dominant Five wing are more introverted, cautious, and withdrawn.

With a stronger Seven wing, Sixes are more playful and adventurous, more active, but they can also be a little impulsive.

The movement of energy for a Six

A happy and secure Six tends to take on the characteristics of a Nine. They are better able to relax, trust themselves, empathize with the group, and see a broader point of view. However, they may overdo recreational drugs, such as alcohol and other substances, or avoid obsessing about fears by sleeping too much.

When they are stressed and anxious they move toward Three and can endanger their health with overwork in an attempt to avoid worries. They may also deceive themselves or others with lies to cover up mistakes or to climb the ladder. On a positive note, they find it easy to acknowledge their achievements.

It helps Sixes to take attention away from thinking, worrying, and running the WPS and to redirect energy into the much neglected body in some way (Helen Palmer, a Six, said she used to think her body ended at her neck). A Six friend of mine used to take a day off from the office and running a business to come and help me in the garden. Taking walks and getting the heart rate pumping is a good way to disperse surplus adrenalin, as is running. Yoga helps to restore calm and flex a tense body, and works on the meridians that control fear.

How Sixes can nurture themselves and grow

- Check out your fears with a trusted friend.
- When fear is overwhelming, drop the attention to the breath in the belly.
- Get your hands in the soil and grow things.
- Do something practical or creative that you find absorbing, such as painting, pottery, sculpting, sewing, and so on.
- Keep a diary in which you honestly write down your fears. Go back after each week and see how many of them were real and how many imagined.
- Keep a separate book in which you record intuitions, and their consequences, to develop a sense of when they are reliable.
- Lighten up by going to funny films and spending time with entertaining friends.
- When fear grips, repeat to yourself like a mantra, "It's going to be OK."
- When someone gives you a compliment, resist your first impulse to reject it, and learn to hear what people value about you.
- Take part in a regular, heart-pumping sport or other physical activity to disperse the adrenalin in your bloodstream that the panic creates.
- Join a yoga class to learn to acknowledge your body. Pay particular attention to the posture given for the Six on pages 118–19.
- Become conscious of your habit of doubting, so that you can choose to transform it by developing faith and courage.

How we can support a Six

- Be honest, clear, and direct.
- Do not dismiss their fears; patiently work through them together.
- Remember the times when you were afraid, and don't judge a Six for their fears.
- Enjoy fun times and laughter with them.
- Help them extend their comfort zone into new areas in a supportive way.
- When they overreact, count to ten. Don't match them.
- Give them plenty of reassurance.
- Don't startle them.
- Encourage them not to work so hard.
- Join them in physical activity that helps them get into their bodies.

"What I like about being a Six"

- The ability to analyze and appreciate the depth and complexity of issues.
- Seeing beneath the surface.
- Always having something to think about.
- The excitement and stimulation of intellectual inquiry.
- The appreciation of being safe in the midst of perceived danger.
- Having lasting friendships of great intimacy and depth.
- Experiencing the joy of things that turn out well.
- Staying calm in the face of disaster.
- My sense of humor.
- My independence.

"What I dislike/find difficult about being a Six"

- Being ambushed by doubt.
- Not always being comfortable with my own authority.
- Getting so nervous and anxious about things.
- Feeling under attack and being sharp in retaliation.
- Missing so much of the present by imagining a difficult future.
- The pattern of self-sabotage.

"How you can help me"

- Take my doubts seriously so that I can question their validity.
- Appreciate me sincerely in a quiet and moderate way, and don't sing my praises too loudly.
- Encourage me to talk about how I am feeling as you are listening to my thinking.
- Demonstrate emotional constancy to support my need to stand firm and be loyal.
- Help me see the effect of my own doubting mind on others.
- Protect yourself from my sharpness long enough to teach me the pleasure of receiving you without claws.
- Make me shake with laughter, not fear.

type seven the epicure

GLUTTONY

Keep on the sunny side of life, always on the sunny side of life.
It will help us every day; it will brighten all the way if we'll keep
on the sunny side of life.

Folk song by Ada Blenkham

Sevens at their best
Optimistic
Enthusiastic
Curious
Entrepreneurial
Imaginative
Spontaneous
Productive
Fun-loving
Charming
Confident

Sevens at their worst
Rebellious
Narcissistic
Scattered
Uncommitted
Undisciplined
Impulsive
Self-destructive
Manic
Over-talkative
Insensitive

Passion
Gluttony

Repeating habit
Rationalizing

Higher mind
Sobriety

Virtue
Constancy

Four people and a baby were lost on top of a mountain wearing scant clothing, dressed for the heat of the day. It was early afternoon, the mists were rolling in, and the small quantity of water they had brought with them had run out. The One, aware that he had the map and had taken a wrong turn, was storming on ahead tight-lipped. The baby, a probable Nine, was fast asleep in the backpack, head on her mother's shoulders, sucking her fingers. The Two was thinking that if they continued downhill they were bound to reach a road eventually, and that she could go off and sweet-talk a local into rescuing the others. The mother, a Seven, was reassuring everyone that all was well, and anyway the baby was breast fed, so no problem on that front. The other Seven was skipping down the mountain, arms out like a plane, singing, "Always look on the bright side of life. . . ." If you are not already convinced, this scenario should help you acknowledge that we do not all react to situations in the same way.

Sevens can be relied on to add a little sparkle to an event; they are the distributors of fairy dust. I've lost count of the number of Enneagram workshops where I've felt the entire room lift as the Seven panel took to the stage and we heard, "Why can't we all be Sevens?" Sevens live on the sunny side of life. If it has cracks, Sevens are the wallpaper on top of them. You have a new Seven friend? Better be ready to attend several different events in the course of a day, dance until dawn, and be up and sparkling with the champagne at breakfast.

This type delights in the smorgasbord of life. They love potluck parties where they can taste a little of everything. A new job, fantastic – but even as they fill in the application form there are likely to be several other options in the pipeline that do not necessarily close with their signature on the contract. When I say that their boredom threshold is low, I am talking ground level.

I will share with you something very interesting that has just happened to me. I write in a little barn at the bottom of my garden, and I just popped up to the house to make myself a mug of green tea. So how come I suddenly find myself in the middle of the raspberry bushes, mug in hand, talking to a tame robin? I will tell you how come. Being a type Two, I tend to merge with the different types as I write about them, and it is typical of a Seven to be easily distracted. The word is "fascination" – Sevens can be fascinated by almost anything.

I was driving along a quiet road with my friend when I saw something by the side of the road that attracted my attention. I asked her to stop. I couldn't take my eyes off it. "Rosi," she said,

"will you just look at yourself? Look at what you're doing – that's a dead squirrel for goodness' sake!"

Sevens have a talent for getting a project up and running. They are ideas people, creative, lateral thinkers. You own a huge record company? Hell, why not buy an airline, or fly a hot-air balloon around the world, and while you are on a roll with transportation, a few trains would be fun. Yes, you've guessed it – entrepreneur Richard Branson displays all the typical traits of a Seven. He has the warm charm, boyish behavior, and "let's-do-it" attitude.

Now, it probably has not struck you at all in what I have written about Sevens so far that they are a Fear type. At the top of the fear triad, Sevens deal with it by going out to play; they rationalize their fear.

Type Seven personalities, when they grew to an age where they became conscious of the terrors that existed in the world around them, protected themselves by pretending they simply didn't exist. Their attention turned to multiple options instead, to dreaming about future plans. When life gets tough, the Sevens get going – off to where they won't have to face the pain and discomfort.

The world of the Seven child seemed limiting, frustrating; the strategy evolved to avoid that pain. They became gluttons for new ideas and for interesting things to do.

I am married, and it's a good marriage – but my wife says it's as if I always have one foot dangling out of the bed.

Rationalization is the key word that applies to Sevens. Try to confront them with their potentially harmful behavior and they will come up with a million reasons why it is not.

I hated my Seven daughter hitchhiking, it worried me sick, but reasoning with her didn't work, and short of physically tying her to the table leg I could see no way to stop her. Money wasn't an issue; I would happily have paid the fare. "I always have interesting experiences when I hitch," she'd say, darting out the door.

Sevens thrive in the type of work situation where they have a large amount of autonomy and the freedom to follow through on their ideas. They are happy working for themselves – as entrepreneurs, for example – and are great at getting new projects off the ground. But just don't expect them to hang around to dot the i's and cross the t's. The minute the task becomes boring they are off to more pleasant pastures, the ones they have been thinking of since they committed to the job. Oops. Did I say commit? A Seven is the Puer Eternus in Jungian terms, the eternal child, and what better example than Peter Pan.

Highly idealistic, they enjoy working for charities, particularly if the organizations concerned are charged with changing the world. Greenpeace, Friends of the Earth, the World Wide Fund for Nature—seventh heaven! They can happily stay in the same job for years at a time, as long as the work provides them with plenty of variety and stimulation.

I have worked as a health visitor for many, many years, but every day is different. I work mostly on my own, driving around visiting families. On any given day I never know what is going to hit me as I walk through the door. I do a lot of child protection work, and sometimes it's very heavy.

Which brings me to a particular affinity Sevens have for working with the dark side of life. There is a project in San Francisco where members of the public support AIDS sufferers in a hospice. Recent research has shown that it is type Sevens who are most likely to stay the course.

I do a lot of grief counseling in my job as a cleric. I go to many funerals. But bereavement is a crisis and that's always quite fun.

Good exemplars of Seven behavior are Groucho Marx, Wolfgang Amadeus Mozart, Walt Whitman, Ram Dass, Tom Robbins, and Thoreau. Their charm and optimism are infectious; it's impossible to be mad with them for long. As children they may frighten you half out of your wits with their death-defying antics, but as adults they can show us the positive side of seeing the world as a place full of supportive, kindly people full of possibilities. Sevens live in a world of serendipitous events, of expansion and good fortune. And if that's how you see the world, it seems the world often rewards you for that view. No problem in that, is there?

Gluttony – the passion for a Seven

The black and white yin/yang symbol represents perfect balance. The white portion represents outgoing energy, action, light, summer, and heaven. The dark portion represents stored inner energy, rest, dark, winter, and earth. In the light portion there is a small black dot; in the dark, a small light dot. The problem for the Seven is that they are missing the black dot. More than that, they are walling off the whole of the dark side and pretending it doesn't exist.

The mother who was worried for her hitchhiking daughter was rightly concerned. Fear is a useful emotion and we all need a measure of it for our protection. And what of other less comfortable emotions? When people are angry with us don't we often learn something of benefit? If someone expresses grief, how might it affect that relationship if we brush off their pain? And what normal human body can keep going at the pace the Seven's denial of discomfort requires?

I was trying to figure out how I could go to the 60th birthday party, and the housewarming, and attend Toby's new play all on the same day when they were scattered all over the map. I managed two of the events, and I had a lot of fun. But I could barely focus by Monday morning. I was utterly exhausted.

Sevens often talk of their energy being run into the ground. It helps them to identify when they are

Type Seven – the dynamic movement of energy

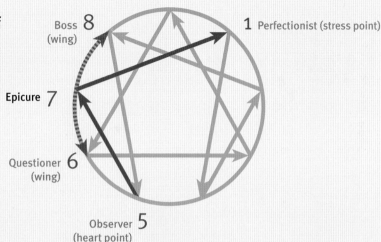

Boss 8 (wing)

1 Perfectionist (stress point)

Epicure 7

Questioner 6 (wing)

Observer 5 (heart point)

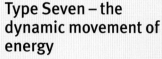

■ Wings
■ Movement of energy

The wings

When a Seven has a stronger Eight wing they are more assertive, confrontational, exuberant, competitive, and materialistic.

A Seven with a stronger Six wing is more responsible, anxious, loyal, and endearing.

The movement of energy for a Seven

A Seven who feels secure moves to the Five space. They are happy spending time alone, in their minds, working on projects and the like. They become more introspective and quieter, and ironically are better able to get in touch with their fears. However, they may become more self-absorbed and reckless.

When a Seven is stressed they move toward the One space and can become forceful to the point of pushiness, and more nit-picking. They become more judgmental of themselves, resentful of restriction and are generally more irritable. They may become obsessive about the project they are working on and lose some of their ability to laugh and be light. To counter this, they will be more productive, more likely to follow a project through to its conclusion, and more altruistic.

packing the schedule too tight and to consider what uncomfortable emotion they might be avoiding. What are they afraid of?

Their blind spot to harm can sometimes depend on the vigilance of well-meaning friends and relatives, who may feel the strain of watching a Seven dice with death.

She hardly ever gave away the fact that she was afraid – but when we were driving around the Australian bush we often stopped off at billabongs right out in the wilds to swim. She'd always say "you go in first, Mom." I knew what that was about. She was worried in case there were any freshwater crocodiles in there, which, although considered harmless to man, can still grow to a toothy 6 feet (2 meters) long.

How Sevens can nurture themselves and grow

- Focus on what you have, rather on what you dream of getting.
- Stitch on your shadow! Include the dark side of your life. Talk about problems with your friends. Look on it as a fascinating adventure into the unknown.
- Regular exercise helps, and should be made routine.
- Yoga exercises that work the back and legs are especially helpful. Steady yourself by doing the Tree posture on pages 120–21.
- Start a journal and include all your feelings, good and bad. Check back through it regularly to see that this is happening. Spend time reflecting on the journal.
- Regulate your meals and sleep. Pay particular attention to this before exhaustion sets in.
- Negotiate quality time with your partner and friends, when you can chill.
- Notice the balance of "talk" to "listen" and make sure you give others air time.
- Notice when you are rationalizing. Ask, "What uncomfortable emotion am I avoiding feeling?"
- Do a regular attention practice/meditation to help you notice when your mind is flying off to future plans and options.
- When the urge to "get going" arises, take a deep breath and make a commitment to finish the project and develop constancy.
- Read only one book at a time – OK, two . . . but just two!
- Feel gratitude daily for all that you have, and affirm that you need not fear lack. You have plenty of all that you need.
- Be conscious of your habit of gluttony to enable yourself to change it, and to invite in the transformation to the opposite – constancy.

How we can support a Seven

- Gently point it out to them when they are taking on too much to the point of exhaustion.
- Suggest it might be interesting to spend some quality thinking time alone.
- Give them plenty of freedom.
- Share fun, exciting adventures with them (you can always pack the bandages).
- Listen to their dreams and visions and support them in their ideas.
- Don't lean on them too much by being needy and dependent.
- Rather than try to change them, appreciate them for the sparkle they bring to your life.
- Don't tell them what to do. Suggest that whatever it is might be a fun, new approach.
- Let them know how much you appreciate their humor.
- Reassure them when they start getting in touch with their dark side.
- Acknowledge the effort they put into commitment when they do.
- Don't beat around the bush – come straight to the point and be brief.

"What I like about being a Seven"

- Being spontaneous.
- Having a sense of adventure and getting out there.

"What I dislike/find difficult about being a Seven"

- There are so many options and I have to make so many choices.

"How you can help me"

- Encourage me to focus and prioritize.
- Help me to take time to be still and to reflect.

type eight the boss

Eights at their best
Protective
Loyal
Energetic
Authoritative
Honest
Fair
Persistent
Direct
Straightforward
Unpretentious
Self-confident

Eights at their worst
Bombastic
Controlling
Aggressive
Insensitive
Rebellious
Anti-authoritarian
Self-centered
Domineering
Skeptical
Contentious
Ruthless

Passion
Lust

Repeating habit
Vengeance

Higher mind
Truth

Virtue
Innocence

LUST

I hate a fellow whom pride, or cowardice, or laziness drives into a corner, and who does nothing when he is there but sit and growl; let him come out as I do and bark.

Samuel Johnson

Push out the boundaries. Wherever you are sitting, or lying, feel an expansion that starts in the belly and moves outward, further and further. Mentally burst through anything that restrains you; feel your energy demolish any confining walls. Nothing stops the expansion; imagine yourself large, like Gulliver in the land of the Lilliputians. Your hands are clenched in tight fists; you are prepared for action. Here to stamp out injustice in the world, you are looking for trouble, for someone to match your energy.

Then you see a mouse in the corner of the room, being toyed with by a cat. You save it, lifting it protectively to your heart. Tenderly, you place the mouse in a safe haven and stand over it like a colossus, daring anyone to come near. Welcome. You have just experienced the energy of a type Eight.

If you have ever been rescued from dire circumstances, or challenged to a bout of arm wrestling in a bar, chances are it was by an Eight.

One day when I took my seven-year-old daughter to school on our bikes, four boys trying to compete to be first through the gate ran her over. My first impulse was not to look after my daughter, but to tell off the selfish culprits.

These are the protectors of the world, helpful people blazing a trail like pioneers, making it safe for others to follow. Tough, combative, challenging, confrontational, Eights are people who are not going to let things lie. Go to Enneagram conferences and listen for them. You will surely hear them long before you see them. If there is a toe-to-toe confrontation going on across a table full of shouting, arguing people, don't be deceived. They love it. Hang around for a few moments longer and you will see them laughing and slapping each other's backs, ordering another round of drinks, relishing the opportunity to match energies. Eights are big-hearted people, magnanimous, generous, and ready to forgive and ask to be forgiven.

Less is not enough; more is hardly touching on it. Too much, too long, too late, too often, too loud … too *anything*! Fast cars, extreme sports, partying until dawn, drinking the rest of us under the table. They have a lust for life. The actor Oliver Reed was a classic example of an Eight, as was Gurdjieff, who fathered the Enneagram in "modern" times. Far be it from him to suggest a little gentle yoga to balance your type. Six and scared? Remember that story of sending them to a graveyard at midnight?

Independent and self-reliant, Eights thrive in situations where they can work on their own initiative and put their leadership skills to the fore. Courageous and bold, they make good soldiers and commanders, company directors, or directors of charities that challenge injustices. They are police officers, ambulance workers, TV newscasters, and journalists – but don't look for them reporting the local village fête, look for them in the war zones. Filmmaker Michael Moore may be an Eight, charging fearlessly into battle with the American gun lobby, rooting out injustice wherever he finds it. Eights have a particular talent for supporting and empowering people – just don't try to challenge them for the top job, or become too needy. They are independent and expect the same of us. They have a nose for manipulation and deceit; better be straight with an Eight. What you see is what you get; they are honest, have abundant energy, and are very hardworking.

We may experience them as hurtful or insensitive, but Eights have no idea how their enormous energy comes across to others. As little children, they held a view that the world is a hard and unjust place where the innocent are taken advantage of, and they learned to become strong and powerful. Respect was earned by being indomitable, imposing their will, and never, ever displaying vulnerability. They were little generals on the family battlefield. And the habit stuck. Attention is placed on what demands immediate action. A lot of energy goes into the control and domination of the people in their orbit. Generally they react rather than respond, which feels too risky. These were the children who kept on playing football with a broken foot, biffed the bully in the eye, and, in many cases, shouldered responsibility for their alcoholic/sick parents.

I hold my tongue and hold my tongue – and then BAM! To me it's fair play. I'll let it go once, twice – but the third time you must expect me to even the score. I say, "Let's put it on the table. What's really on your mind?" If it diverges from moral law it gets me angry. You might need time in a recovery home. Then I'll have compassion. No, if it goes for a third time, you want a fight. Call a witness, because I'll smack you on the nose.

That may sound a bit extreme, but we are talking Eight here, so we are in the territory of the extreme. Fair-minded, persistent, truthful, straightforward, and unpretentious – we could all learn from the Eights about defending ourselves and facing challenges. Not easy then in all this bluster to see the cream puffs that they really are (remember that mouse in the opening paragraphs?). That armor that protects a core of vulnerability is hard for us to penetrate. Their bodies often do look armored, their muscles held in readiness. Their upper bodies and arms are often over-contracted or over-developed, their eyes "don't-mess-with-me" fierce.

Look at the roll call of famous Eights to get an idea of how strong they are: Henry VIII (an excess of wives!), Pablo Picasso, Gurdjieff, Madame Blavatsky, Sean Penn, Nietzsche, Golda Meir, Ludwig van Beethoven, Charles de Gaulle, Helmut Kohl, John Wayne, Sarah Ferguson, and Bette Midler.

Lust – the passion for an Eight

The trouble with all this lustful energy, outwardly expressed, is the misunderstandings that can arise, the unevenness of the personality. If what others see is a raging bull, pounding through any ideas they might have, tossing weaker individuals out of the way with their horns, most people will take the behavior at face value and will not stop to consider that there might be an underlying vulnerability.

If Sevens wall off the dark side of life, then Eights wall off vulnerability. Sometimes it is not only their vulnerability that is getting dismissed – it might be ours as well. For although Eights make wonderful protectors, they can also be very intolerant of perceived weakness in others, or error, and can be heedless and dismissive of others' views.

The lust can be literal; serial affairs that destroy a marriage, for example, although few take it to the extremes of Henry VIII. The seeking out of conflict can terrorize a partner, especially if that partner is someone who prefers to avoid confrontation – a Fear type, for example. The habit of attention that goes toward seeking vengeance can get them into all sorts of trouble.

I once pushed my brother so hard against the kitchen wall that the tiles broke. I got that angry because he stole some pieces of meat I was cutting up for the spaghetti sauce.

Lucky it wasn't the knife!

The burden for the Eight of feeling that they have to save the world can overwhelm them at times. When I did my Enneagram training in Palo Alto, in the United States, I was watching a panel of body types (Eights, Ones, and Nines) when there was a minor earthquake. The counterphobic Six leading the panel denied it was an earthquake and insisted it was a passing train. This Two thought, "I'll head for the door when the rest of them do. This is California after all – they'll know." But the Eight on the panel was traumatized. She thought she had to protect everybody in the whole room, some 40 people or more.

Lust can leak into other more dangerous areas; it is all too easy for the Eight to dive down the neck of a bottle or to use recreational drugs in a thirst for the extreme. They love a good drinking binge into the small hours. The cars may be just a little too fast and dangerous, the tightrope too high.

Revenge is sweet to the Eight:

If I see a slow car waiting to be allowed into the line of traffic I take great delight in waving it in in front of me. It makes the other drivers on my tail mad. I can get my own back for them pushing me.

If everyone perceives you as the strong one, or the domineering personality, this reinforces the body armor and gives the Eight less opportunity to express their vulnerability, and they may feel the inner dissatisfaction of being misunderstood. They may find themselves surrounded by people who assume that the assertive Eight is making a personal attack on them, which can lead to all manner of problems, both at work and at home. It is hard for them when they scare people away with their bluntness, when it was unintentional. Although making an impact, they are not out to impress.

Type Eight – the dynamic movement of energy

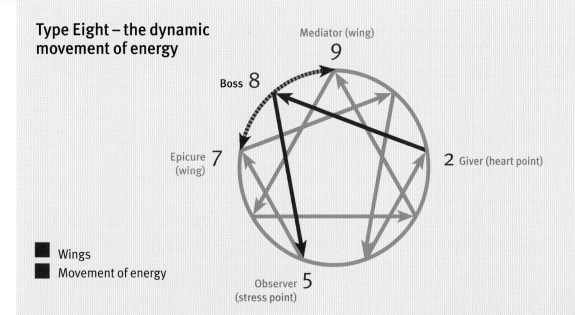

Wings
Movement of energy

The wings

An Eight with a stronger Seven wing is more playful, entrepreneurial, extroverted, energetic, egocentric, and speedy.

An Eight with a stronger Nine wing is more laid-back, inclusive, and with a less overt, quiet strength. They are gentler and more receptive.

The movement of energy for an Eight

When Eights are feeling happy and secure they tend to move to the energy of a Two and are better able to show vulnerability. It is easier for them to love and receive love. They are also more attuned to others' needs. However, they can become needier, possessive, and overreact defensively.

An Eight when stressed tends to withdraw to type Five. Here they can turn their anger in on themselves; experiencing themselves as hopeless, and believing themselves bad, debauched, they think, why bother? Detached from their feelings, they can become afraid that others are turning against them, feel defeated and depressed. On the other hand, they are able to be more objective and to think twice before acting.

How Eights can nurture themselves and grow

- Develop spatial and energy awareness with the close observation of your body developed by regular yoga practice, particularly the forward bend on pages 122–23.
- Develop a habit of listening to other people's points of view.
- Get feedback from friends or family on how forcefully your comments come across.
- Look for what you appreciate in others and tell them regularly.
- Keep a pile of old crockery in the shed ready to smash against a wall when you need to release pent-up anger safely.
- Start a pattern of relinquishing control in a small way, in certain areas of your life, and become accustomed to going with the flow.
- Express your need for affection openly. Observe that showing vulnerability does not compromise your strength – it enhances it.
- Seek out anger-management courses/groups so that you have a strategy in place to deal with it when you need it.
- Join a rehabilitation program if substance abuse is your issue.
- Learn to meditate and to become the observer of your anger, rather than being engaged with it, and start to enjoy the peace within.
- Notice when lust or the need for vengeance arises, how it feels in your body, and what it makes you do, so that you can choose not to go with it in order to invite transformation to its opposite, the virtue of innocence.

How we can support an Eight

- Be trustworthy, honest, and straight with them.
- When they need to be alone, give them the space.
- Don't assume it's a personal attack if they are ranting. It's just the way they are.
- They will sniff out mere flattery and not be impressed by it.
- Match their energy and stand up for yourself to earn their respect.
- If you have been vulnerable, and they protected you, show your appreciation.
- Stand up for them when people misinterpret them.
- Help them soften their bodies with massage and walks in the countryside.
- Show them you respect them more than ever when they do express vulnerability.
- Give them feedback on their intensity when they have affected you strongly.

"What I like about being an Eight"

- I am strong and protective of other people, especially those who find it less easy to stand up for themselves. I can help them have confidence in themselves. I like making the way ahead safe for others.
- I am like a two-edged sword – honest and direct – and like others to be the same.
- People know where they stand with me.
- I do not experience danger or fear.
- As others get to know me (beneath what appears a hard shell) they will find someone who is big-hearted and giving, generous with time and whatever else there is.
- I am hardworking and have high energy, and I am more likely to react than necessarily see what is coming.
- I am ready to confront a lack of fairness or justness.

"What I don't like about being an Eight"

- I can be naive (rather than "innocent").
- Others see me as insensitive when, in truth, I can feel easily rejected.
- Because of my directness, I am seen as abrupt and abrasive – even rude.
- The way I hide my weakness and vulnerability.
- Because of my focused and narrow attention style, I find it difficult to see the wider perspectives.
- I experience myself as "bad" and "hopeless" and therefore have difficulty accepting the positive from others.
- I hide my vulnerability and weaker side, so I am hard to get through to. This is as true for other Eights as it is for me.

"How you can help me"

- When I am angry, confront me. Don't go away.
- Don't patronize me, but meet me as an equal.
- Hug me. Eights are body types and need and love body contact.
- Tell me openly and honestly if I did hurt you – but do it two days after the outburst.

type nine the mediator

SLOTH

*Once upon a time in Spain there was a little bull and his name
was Ferdinand.*
*All the other little bulls he lived with would run and jump and butt their heads
together; but not Ferdinand.*
He liked to sit just quietly and smell the flowers.

Munro Leaf *Ferdinand the Bull*

Nines at their best

Excellent mediators
Reassuring
Nonjudgmental
Patient
Peaceful
Receptive
Empathetic
Generous
Gentle
Pleasant

Nines at their worst

Stubborn
Obsessive
Passive-Aggressive
Spaced out
Nonassertive
Absent-minded
Apathetic
Judgmental
Forgetful
Overly
accommodating

Passion
Sloth

Repeating habit
Indolence

Higher mind
Love

Virtue
Right action

Slow the pace right down now as you enter the world of the Nine. Sit comfortably in your chair, slump a little, and when you next get up and move, walk more slowly and let life come to you rather than chasing after it.

I enjoy seeing what comes rather than going out and getting. You're in your own mental groove when you just sit and relax. It could be anything, or anybody that comes to you, and that's kind of interesting.

Let impressions waft over you like gentle, puffy clouds on a warm day. People, objects, ideas, and places lead you toward them, each one equally absorbing. A woman sits beside you on a park bench and starts talking; you are friendly and attentive, stroking her dog. Before long you are into a conversation about dachshunds, about why this breed became the shape it is. An hour passes before you notice that you'll miss your 10 A.M. appointment if you don't get a move on.

On the way there you smell the aroma of fresh coffee coming from a little café on the corner. Soon you find yourself enjoying a fat slice of cheesecake with a man from Cuba, discussing the political situation there. The expert on dachshunds has shape-shifted into an expert on Cuban politics; he mirrors his companion, as if he has somehow merged with him. But Nines do not merge the way a Two does. Nines are unselective; it is merely a question of who happens to be sitting next to them at the time.

It is hard for a Nine to stay on track. Send a Nine out with a shopping list of 15 items, most not essential, but at the top of the list, and underlined, is a vital item – guess what doesn't get bought? Things do get done, more often than not, but mostly at the eleventh hour. Accounts are done at midnight the day before the deadline, when finally a surge of energy will win through.

Nines have global vision. Watch their arms as they talk, waving around in circles. They are considering all the opinions, pros and cons, perspectives, cultural differences. Nines are good listeners and are well suited to the caring professions – as counselors, for example. Look for them in the United Nations, or negotiating peace in Iraq, or in Northern Ireland putting their mediation skills and diplomacy to good use. They fare better with a structured routine and are reassured by their habits. They tend to thrive in more structured professions, as bureaucrats, teaching, or in the civil service. They don't

want to be identified with one stance to the exclusion of others, however.

I began with one tattoo, the yin/yang symbol. I wanted to include Islam, so I had another done just above it. But what about Christianity? I added a cross, the Indian "Om" symbol … and the Tibetan Om Mani Padme Hung….

The tendency of not taking a position can be crippling for the Nine. Would she like an Indian meal or Italian? How about that new bistro in the mall? Easier to go with the flow and let the others decide. If you see a Nine looking sad, it is often because they feel that their opinion was ignored – the downside of never taking a stand. Let me give you a tip. They often know what they don't want to do and can make a decision if presented with only two choices.

Friendly, helpful, equitable people, the Nines are ever ready to search the Internet for that latest gadget for you, or for a recipe for bread pudding. Next day it is on your desk – they eventually tracked it down in a bookshop after a few hours searching for it on the Net. If pashminas were made for Fours, the Internet was made for Nines. They are generous with their knowledge, so you had better not be in a hurry if you ask a question of a Nine.

I asked my husband the time. I got the time in Paris, the time in Hong Kong, the time in New York, and a long lecture on the concept of time. Half an hour later I still didn't know what time it was.

It is almost impossible for a Nine to say no. To say no is to risk rejection by that person, and to lose the perfect union that they seek.

Nines may not look angry, but anger is their issue. In their case the anger is unacknowledged (they often claim they never get angry) or projected onto someone else. If it does find expression, it more usually comes out passively, in stubbornness. Taking a long, slow bath while you twiddle your thumbs waiting to take her to the restaurant is a pretty strong clue that she wasn't that eager to go out in the first place.

Hating conflict, Nines distance themselves from their anger by unconsciously delegating it to others. We all have our work cut out with the uncomfortable side of our Enneagram type: when a Nine eventually acknowledges their anger, the real growth can begin. The temptation, instead, is to overindulge in food, drink, or whatever, to avoid unpleasantness: not the best way to honor their intuition center, the gut. The skillful way is to notice the hand moving toward the cake and to preempt it by breathing into the gut, and asking for guidance for what it is making them angry that they are trying to avoid.

I've learned to look inside myself when someone is angry with me, to find my own unexpressed anger. It takes a lot to make me angry, but what sure does it is if people are angry with me. I feel their anger is unjustified and it makes me feel rebellious as a result. It was really difficult at first to own it – me, angry?

The peace-loving Nine will fire off angry letters to the utility board, take on the phone company, anything rather than shout at the person who has just ignored them. Better to keep them waiting while you float in scented bath water. In this way, the passive Nines can be experienced as controlling.

Nines are generally good in groups and gain energy there, and they are also good team players. The qualities they bring to a group are consideration, gentleness, inclusiveness, and mediation. Mikhail Gorbachev is a good example of a Nine politician. Ringo Starr of the former Beatles is probably a Nine, and so is the singer Luciano Pavarotti. The filmmaker Alfred Hitchcock was a Nine.

Sloth – the passion for a nine

If you can see all the options, and there are so many, how on earth do you choose which one to take? If, while you lie on the deck chair, the grass is crying out to be mown, the shed painted, and the hedge trimmed, and all have equal significance, what do you do? Why, nothing at all, of course.

He went inside to do his accounts; he was way behind with them already. A couple of hours later I took him a cup of tea. There he was, doing his accounts, fast asleep on the sofa.

The Nine who didn't want to go to the restaurant and just went along with the flow was slothful about expressing her own needs. Sometimes it's easier to do the same thing over and over again.

Whenever I go out for a meal I choose the same thing: chicken. It saves having to make a choice. I can still talk about it, compare it with chicken I've eaten at different restaurants in the past, whether it was cooked better here or there, if the skin was crisper or the sauce more piquant, or whatever. There's just as much opportunity to talk about the meal as there would be if I'd chosen something different.

If you think you are nagging a slothful Nine, don't worry – they can do it perfectly well for themselves. They know the job needs doing, they know they will get around to it eventually, but when they lay their head next to yours on the pillow at night and the job is still not done, they feel the sadness of time slipping by.

I just wish she would trust me that I will get around to doing that job she asked me to do. It's just that it might not be right away. Of course I will do it – eventually.

There is frequently an aura of sorrow around the Nine of agendas not followed, opportunities missed, and relationships slipping by. This is an old pattern – the Nine child often felt neglected, almost invisible in the family. The weight of this self-forgetting settles on them like a heavy mantle, giving an air of fatigue, of inertia.

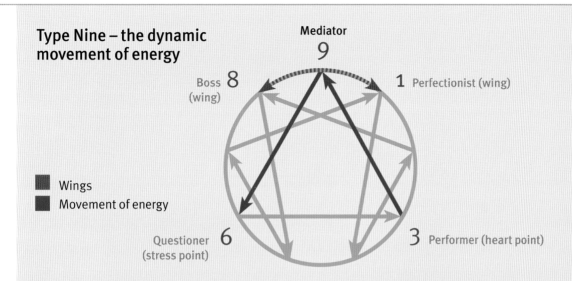

Type Nine – the dynamic movement of energy

Mediator
9

Boss **8** (wing)

1 Perfectionist (wing)

■ Wings
■ Movement of energy

Questioner **6** (stress point)

3 Performer (heart point)

The wings

A tilt to their Eight wing provides a Nine with more energy than a tilt to the One wing. Here they are better able to assert themselves, and are more outgoing – if a bit more rebellious. However, there may be some conflict between being assertive and being a peacemaker.

Nines with a stronger One wing are more judgmental and nit-picking, as well as more emotionally controlled.

The movement of energy for a Nine

When a Nine feels good they move to the positive side of Three, the Performer. You see them get into action, becoming performers, and being far more focused. Nines in this mode make excellent teachers. On the downside, they can take on too much and begin to feel overwhelmed.

A Nine in stress moves to the Six space: "Why are you asking me to do this? Why should I trust the head teacher?" However, this point provides useful energy to express their own needs, and to be more businesslike and realistic about how to achieve things.

There's always a mass of things in the way between me and what I really want to do. My mind looks like a cluttered room full of boxes stuffed with memos. I'm scurrying between the piles, trying to get a little bit of each thing done before one of the piles topples over on me. It looks like nothing is getting done from the outside, but that's because I'm running between piles of too many things to do on the inside.

The trap for the rest of us is to get hooked into trying to sort out the Nine's life, to try to guide their direction. But be warned – it is not easy to motivate a Nine, no matter how well intended you may be. On a lighter note, the Nines talk of experiencing great peace in their union with man and nature.

The sense of just being is utterly absorbing. I can lie there looking up at the clouds passing by and feel so at one with the universe it's hard even to contemplate moving. Hours can go by, and nothing can seem more important to do.

How Nines can nurture themselves and grow

- Take regular exercise that gets the heartbeat going and amps up the energy.
- Practice asking clearly for what you want in relationships.
- If you find yourself saying, "I don't know," or "OK, whatever . . . " pay attention. Instead tell them you will let them know when you decide, but that you need time to think.
- Go to the belly center and listen when someone is getting angry with you.
- Start a daily journal. Every day write down, "I am angry about . . . " at least three times and learn to acknowledge this emotion in your life.
- Make daily realistic lists of what you want to accomplish and stick to them.
- If you go to the fridge between meals, ask what uncomfortable thing you are avoiding.
- Learn to include your opinion in a group by asking your higher self what it wants, as if it were another equally valid member, and verbalize it.
- If you find yourself becoming judgmental, ask, "What am I angry about?"
- Enjoy relaxing times in your day, but make them part of the structure and give them a time limit – if necessary set a timer.
- Get your friends to come along with you when you take up a new hobby.
- Do the Salute to the Sun sequence on pages 124–25 every morning before breakfast.
- Become aware of sloth toward your own agenda so that you can work to invite in, with love and respect for yourself, the transformation to its opposite – right action.

How we can support a Nine

- Be patient, giving time for them to express their opinion, even if it means waiting a day.
- Be gentle with any feedback; they are most sensitive to criticism.
- Don't lay a lot of pressure or expectation on a Nine if you ask them to do something.
- Praise them when they have done a job well; show them that you have noticed.
- Nines warm to physical affection; it helps them get in touch with their feelings.
- Share quiet times with them watching the grass grow.
- Learn to trust that the job will get done, and give them time to do it.
- Don't take advantage of the Nine's willingness to help when you see it is distracting them from their own agenda.
- Be sure to mention it when they are looking good to you.
- Be patient when they are talking. Let them take the time they need to make their point.

"What I like about being a Nine"

- I like the fact that not a lot bothers me.
- I can imagine what it's like from other people's points of view.
- Being in touch with my own stillness.
- Watching grass grow, the clouds change shape, other people.
- Loving everything without wanting to change it, affect it, or need to get involved with it.
- The ability to allow myself to be swept along by other people without any effort.

"What I dislike/find difficult about being a Nine"

- Not knowing what to do.
- Lack of self-motivation.
- "Possible" missed opportunities.
- Times of helplessness.
- Inability to cope in high-pressure environments.
- Being too sensitive to other people's moods and what they say about me.

"How you can help me"

- Allow significant pauses in conversation to allow me to gather my thoughts.
- Ask me what I think, how I feel. But give me the time, alone if necessary, to reply.
- Don't blame me for your frustration or impatience.
- Be careful not to off-load to me for too long at a stretch.
- Do things together.
- Forgive me for drifting off sometimes; it's nothing personal.
- Give me some time to be slow or peaceful, or to be by myself, at least once a day.
- If I am not doing what you want, you need to ask what is going on in a gentle way, rather than apply pressure.
- Before criticizing me, always appreciate something about me first.

CHAPTER TWO

The five elements

Your life expresses itself through
your body and your mind.

*Your body is our visible spirit: it is the
miracle of spirit made manifest.*

Yogi Amrit Desai

introduction to the elements

We now come to new territory for the Enneagram: the five elements of classical Chinese acupuncture, and their emotional, physical, and spiritual associations with the 12 main meridians, and the nine types. After introducing each element I make practical suggestions for simple lifestyle changes that, although beneficial to all types, are exceptionally so for some.

For many years, a physical approach to working with the Enneagram has been neglected. This has left people who learn more easily through their bodies, and who wish to balance the more mental approach, frustrated. By sharing what I know about the workings of the meridians and how they affect us psychologically, physically, and spiritually, and how we can activate them through the application of yoga postures and meditations, and by living in harmony with nature, I hope to correct this situation. I offer many practical suggestions of how you can work on your type behavior with postures, meditations/visualizations, and by making simple adjustments to how you live. I hope this will open a whole new avenue of growth for experienced students of the Enneagram, and a holistic approach for people who are new to its workings.

Living your life according to the laws of the five elements releases untold potential for personal health on all levels. There is much benefit to be gained by being in harmony with the seasons, and with your body's natural rhythms. Modern lifestyles have separated us from the things that nourish our spirit; it is time to reconnect.

The meridians

Almost 5,000 years ago in China, healers, having observed people closely for hundreds of generations, noticed that there were dynamic pathways of energy that coursed through the body. Further, the healers realized that these energetic pathways related not only to our physical organs and their functions, but also to our emotions. It is believed that they discovered these energy pathways through making a connection between where exactly in the body people had been wounded in battle and subsequent problems they experienced with particular organs and emotions as a result of their injuries.

The ancient healers mapped the energy pathways and called them meridians, which translates from the Chinese as "warp" (as in the warp and weft of a fabric), giving us a beautiful image of our bodies woven in lines of energy. The 12 main meridians each have their own pathway, and interconnect forming a continuous circuit. This is very important. It means that when one meridian is freed of blocks, all 11 others benefit. They work together like a team. Find the team member who is slacking, or acting in a dysfunctional way, give him what he needs to make his recovery, and the entire team breathes a collective sigh of relief. The Chinese referred to these team members (meridians) as "officials" and saw them working together under the rule of the king (the heart meridian) to run the palace (our bodies and our emotions) smoothly.

To have an idea of how this might operate in your body, imagine that there is a severe, unexpected accident or illness to the head of state of the country you live in. Whatever your affiliations, you would experience some degree of shock. In the same way, people who survive heart attacks often go through a period of great confusion and lack of confidence while the ruling heart meridian rebuilds its power.

We can manage the energy in the meridians to our advantage, not only with acupuncture treatments, which require an outside agent with needles, but also by working on them ourselves by doing certain yoga postures, and by doing them with right attention.

Chi – the energy of the meridians

The energy that runs in the meridians is known as Chi (Chee) or Qi (Key) in the Far East, Prana in India, and the Life Force in the West – shown in paintings as a halo of light around the head of Christ or the saints. Clairvoyants can see this aura not just around our heads but surrounding the entire body in an egg shape extending out about 3 feet (1 meter) or more. Our aura is literally colored by our emotions. Were any of us to start looking for it on a regular basis we, too, would see it – animals certainly do. They know when we are afraid, friendly, or hostile. Have you ever felt that someone, a stranger maybe, is standing too close for comfort? That is because they have entered your aura at a time when you are not ready to receive them, or because they are giving off negative energy. (Think of the times when you entered someone's house and sensed that a fight had just taken place.) On the other hand, there are people who seem calm and balanced, their whole being glowing with energy, their very presence seeming to radiate love far beyond their physical being. This is the "Shen," or spirit, shining through their aura.

It is my belief that the ancient healers saw the meridians, and the acupuncture points where they could be stimulated, as well as sensing them. I once watched with fascination a line of light glowing along the pathway of the meridian I had just needled, traveling from the point up the patient's leg. I asked her, without any hint of what I was seeing, "Can you see that?" And I received confirmation when she replied, "You mean that line of light up my leg?" We watched in some awe until it gradually faded over a period of five or six minutes.

As we grow older, unless we pay attention to our physical, spiritual, and emotional needs, our personality permeates our bodies and settles into the structure, and the free flow of Chi is blocked. For instance, when we hold onto a negative emotion, such as fear or anger, it begins to affect our body. The saying goes that after the age of 40 we get the face that we deserve. I would extend this and say that we also get the body we deserve, but would add an optimistic note: to a large extent we can reverse the effect. By working on our bodies, ironing out

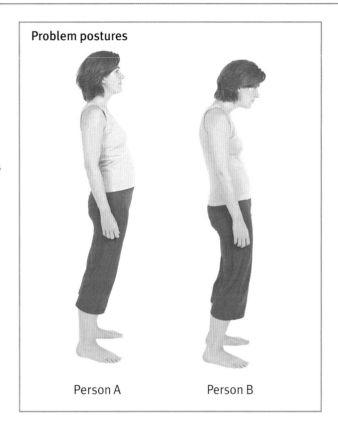

Problem postures

Person A   Person B

the knots and kinks made by our habit of attention, with stretching exercises and meditation, we also work on our psyche.

Look at the images above. Most of us can read what people's habit of attention has been who stand like this. It may even be in conflict with their current emotion and give us the wrong impression of how they are feeling.

PERSON A leads from the belly. The posture shows someone who displays confidence, maybe to the point of over-dominance. The stomach muscles will slacken in time, making the belly protrude, and the muscles in her back will shorten to hold this posture. The responses to this person, who might be an Eight, will be to someone of supreme confidence. What people may miss is the soft center and vulnerability. But if this person practices a lot of forward bends, releasing the tight muscles in the small of the back and tightening those of the stomach, not only will she begin to feel more balanced, but people will respond to her more appropriately. She may find that her ideas are received more willingly, so establishing a positive cycle.

PERSON B is a thinker, a mental type who leads with her head. Life is weighing heavily on these shoulders. The chest is contracting with fear and lack of confidence. The muscles and ligaments are like the guy ropes of the body, holding her in this position even when she relaxes. But movements to stretch the shortened muscles across the chest and contract the slackened muscles of the shoulders will straighten her body, which will then project a more confident image. The result for Person B will be a more positive response from others and increased confidence. She will literally "square up" to people.

Emotions and the meridians

It is common knowledge in the Far East that there is a link between unbalanced emotions and physical dysfunction, and it has been recognized instinctively in the West and is imbedded in our language. There is an old expression that says, "She's got a liver on 'er" to describe an angry woman. Or we say so-and-so "galls" us, meaning that they make us angry. (The liver and the gallbladder meridians control the expression of anger.)

In these modern times, provided that there is adequate shelter, clean water, nutritious food, and protective clothing, the causes of disease are most likely to be internal, occurring as a result of stress and either an excess of certain emotions or a lack of them. When our type behavior is at its least conscious and at its most compulsive, we risk having our emotions tip us over into ill health, as well as disrupt our relationships. One of the ways we can become more conscious of our type behavior is to pay closer attention to our body and how our emotions affect it.

The Enneagram types divide into three groups of three. These relate to core emotional issues: the anger types – Nines, Ones, and Eights; the fear types – Sixes,

The three triads

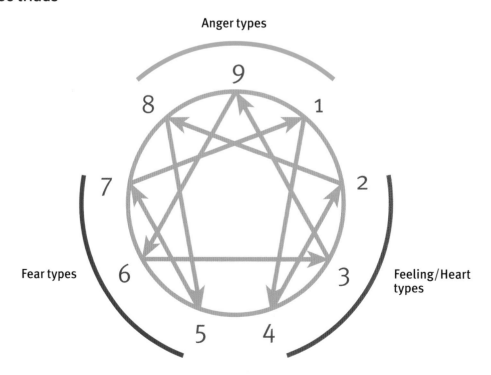

Anger types

9
8   1

7   2

Fear types   6   3   Feeling/Heart types

5   4

Fives, and Sevens; and the feeling types – Threes, Twos, and Fours (see the diagram). For those of you having difficulty identifying your type, the elements and their associations often give a strong clue about the areas in which you should be looking.

The 12 main meridians divide into five elements: Fire, Earth, Metal, Water, and Wood. The emotions of these elements are, respectively: Joy, Sympathy, Grief, Fear, and Anger. Although the fit is not perfect, as I said in the general introduction and history, I found again and again in my many years working as a five-element acupuncturist, primarily on a psychological and spiritual level, that balancing the meridians and their elements also balanced a patient's personality. Patients became happier people, more able to face life with renewed strength, and almost as an added bonus, their physical symptoms got better, too. Often, a conversation would run along the lines of, "How's your knee?" "Oh, that. It got better weeks ago."

The causative factor

There is the same debate in acupuncture circles as there is in the Enneagram community: nurture or nature? Are we born with our type, or did our upbringing make us the way we are?

Everyone has one element that is the key to the harmonious functioning of his or her body/mind/spirit. Further, there is usually a particular meridian that is the key. This primary imbalance is called the causative factor. When that element is treated with due consideration, there is harmony and balance. The trouble is that for many of us our lives have become far removed from what is harmonious for the body/mind/spirit. We stretch our bodies to the limit by staying up after dark in winter, drinking toxins (coffee is toxic to the liver), overworking, and ignoring our relationships and our social lives.

I believe, as I do of our Enneagram type, that we are born with a propensity for problems in one particular element. It is all part of that map we enter the world with. My suggestion is that you read about the five elements with an open mind, as you did the previous

chapter on the nine types, as to where you fit. It may be that you are stuck in anger, for example, and that you are unable to express it, but it may not necessarily be your primary issue. There may have been exceptional stress to a particular element. (For example, Earth will be affected if you had a cold and distant or smothering mother.)

You might find that a current situation needs looking at through a certain element, and can be healed through the appropriate postures/lifestyle changes, even if it does not directly relate to your Enneagram type or your element type. We are multi-faceted beings, and all five element energies apply to us and work as a team. A truly balanced body/mind/spirit should experience harmony in all five.

In the following descriptions of the elements, I deal more with the psychological and spiritual problems that may arise than the physical, because the physical problems are easy to imagine. They are associated with the pathway of the meridian, or with the organ itself and its function. For instance, stress to the Wood Element (gall bladder and liver meridians) may cause hepatitis, liver cancer, gallstones, eye problems, tendonitis, knee problems, and so on.

Each element has an associated color, sound, odor, and emotion. Where the emotions, color, or tone of voice are concerned, they relate to an excess or a lack.

When you have read about all five elements, look in the mirror for the color around your eyes and mouth, listen to the sound of your own voice on tape, smell the armpits of yesterday's shirt (sorry, but this does work), and see if you can tell. These are things that people in ancient times, who lived lives more attuned to nature, would have experienced instinctively, and in time you, too, can recognize them.

Think about your predominant emotion: are you angry/too passive, happy/joyless, sympathetic/unsympathetic, stuck in grief, or excessively fearful/fearless? If all five indicators match – for example, if you are green around the eyes and mouth, have a shouting voice (or a faint one), smell rancid, and feel angry or fail to express it, then Wood is your element.

the wood element

Season

Have you ever found it difficult to stick to your New Year's resolutions? And have you ever considered how much more effective they might be if we made them at the true start of the year – in spring? This is when the dormant energy of the earth wakes up and there is enormous potential for growth, renewal, change, and expansion.

In spring, a blade of grass will crack concrete to grow. Seeds that have rested dormant, storing their energy during winter, will split and push up shoots in response to increasing light levels and warmth. Leaves unfurl in the sunshine, spring rains feed the growth, and the stored energy of the winter months is suddenly in action. This is the true birth of the year, and it is the season when the Wood Element has the most energy.

If we are healthy and balanced in body/mind/spirit we, too, feel this burst of positive energy, this sense of optimism and renewal. Overnight, when the seasons change, we should find ourselves full of plans and new projects.

Change is in the air. (One of the clues I had as to when exactly we had moved into spring would be seeing that change in my patients.) In spring we may find ourselves no longer willing to endure restrictions we had formerly accepted; we want to change jobs or relationships, fix things that are broken. Gardeners find the motivation to get out into the air and dig, the do-it-yourself stores are full, cobwebs are dusted down, and jobs that have hung over us for months suddenly can wait no longer. Some of us may even take up banners and march for a cause. You only have to watch the news at this time of the year to see the energy of the Wood Element motivating the human spirit.

If you love spring and are energized only then, or if you lack motivation at this time of year, you may have an imbalance in Wood. Think of all the manifestations of Wood: stems that bend with the wind, brittle sticks, strong branches, trees that grow tall and strong, spindly saplings. Wood Element people can reflect any one of these.

Emotion

Anger, governed by the Wood Element, when it is appropriate, is a positive emotion. It helps us make the changes in our lives that are necessary for our growth. We have many names for the varying degrees of anger we can feel: irritation, annoyance, gall, pique, resentment, fury, exasperation, rage, outrage, wrath. If somebody threatened one of my children, it would be entirely appropriate for me to feel the most intense form of anger from this list. What would not be appropriate, however, would be to respond passively and thereby allow the child to come to harm. If someone turns up half an hour late for an appointment, then it is appropriate for me to feel pique – outrage would be an overreaction unless that person made a regular habit of being late for appointments.

Now let us look at how this element can affect the Enneagram types: what of the One child, planted in a family where she can never get anything right, where the outer critic is constantly on her back? Combine it with a habit of attention that tends to look for fault. The liver and the gallbladder control the ligaments and tendons; anger may make her body rigid, tense, and inflexible. The mind tends to follow. Decisions can become a torment driven by the inner critic: "What if I get it wrong? What if I choose these boots today, and find that I should have chosen the others?" Or: "I'm the only one around here who gets it right. Why should I have to always put in the extra hours to sort things out?" Being stuck in that type of dialog is destined to put an enormous strain on the gallbladder. And because the liver meridian, which is yin, is paired with the yang gallbladder, it will begin to suffer as well.

The Wood Element supports our growth if those meridians are healthy and functioning well. But what of the frustration of plans thwarted, when circumstances restrict us? A plant that grows in acid soil will never thrive in alkaline. A gardener would have to plan where to transplant it for it to flourish, and also decide when would be the most appropriate time to make the move. The frustrations, the stress of not living the life that is appropriate for you, takes its toll on the gallbladder and the liver meridians and, in time, will affect the Wood Element. Before long there will be an inappropriate expression of anger. The cat will get it. Work may suffer. Relationships certainly will.

For the Eight, attuned to the injustices in the world, how does it feel when he cannot solve them all? Or when others have their own ideas about how they might be solved, and when these conflict? The liver begins to pay the price. It may translate into eye problems or sudden sharp pains in the rib cage, dizziness, or even liver cancer. It can also trigger anger at a level beyond what is appropriate.

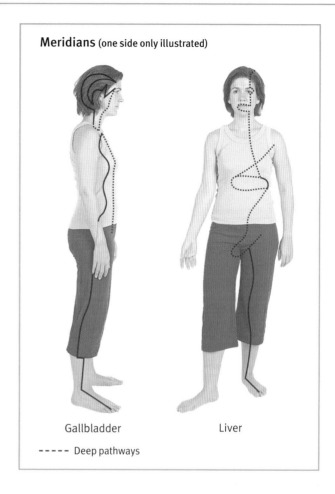

Meridians (one side only illustrated)

Gallbladder   Liver

- - - - - Deep pathways

The Nine, who feels anger more usually at the level of frustration and expresses it through passive aggression, displays the "lack of" this emotion. On the outside there is the appearance of placid compliance and reasonableness; inside, however, their blood may be boiling that they have been overlooked. Anger expressed openly in this case would be an enormous benefit, galvanizing the Nine into action – putting the plant in the best position to thrive.

Meridians – liver and gallbladder
The liver organ, apart from its duty of detoxing and storing the blood, has another function: planning. Physically the liver is connected with the eyes and with sight – on a psychological level it is connected with foresight. You can think of this meridian as the planning official of the palace. The gallbladder meridian, on a

psychological level, is the official chiefly responsible for all the decision-making processes.

If you think about that springtime renewal of energy, you can see how much of it relates to our ability to make plans and decisions. After the slough of winter, when the fog lifts, we are suddenly able to see ahead with much more clarity – action is appropriate.

Color

The color that manifests on the face is usually so subtle that until you look for it specifically you will probably be unaware of its existence. The Impressionist painters certainly recognized the colors on the face and painted them. Once you start looking you will soon see them, too. When an element is out of balance the colors appear first around the eyes and the mouth; the colors emanate from the face, rather than being part of the form. When the Wood Element is out of balance, or when a person is angry, this color will be green. (One of the best ways to start identifying this color is to observe the face of an alcoholic. It may not be just the eyes; rather the whole face may take on a greenish hue.)

Sound

The sound of voice that relates to the Wood Element is said to be shouting, or "lack of" shout. It may be a real shout, or a type of clipped tone in which every syllable is emphasized clearly. But it can also be a faint voice that you are constantly straining to hear. It's often the voice that you hear above all others when you enter a crowded party. Think of that strident tone of the former British prime minister Margaret Thatcher, the voice she tried so hard to train to be softer. It still came out as an angry-sounding whisper. She is an example of a One relating to an appropriate element – Wood. And interestingly, she had to have an operation to release contracted tendons in her hands, and has also had eye problems as well as a stroke, all conditions related to Wood.

Odor

We none of us like to think that we smell, and with deodorants this is no longer the issue that it once was.

However, like the subtle emanation of color from the face, we all have our individual odor that relates to our primary imbalance. The odor may change when we are in a particular mood, but there is always a background smell to a greater or lesser degree. (You should not necessarily feel bad about this; it is actually one of the things that your partner may unwittingly be attracted to.) The odor for the Wood Element is rancid. It is a kind of sharp, slightly acrid smell, similar to the smell of rancid butter. Next time someone loses it in your presence, take a surreptitious sniff.

Time of day

All 12 main meridians have a peak functioning time for two hours each day, followed by a two-hour low in energy some 12 hours later. The gall bladder meridian, with its role as decision-maker, has a peak functioning time for two hours from 11 P.M. Chi energy (the Wei Chi), which circulates over the surface of the body during the day protecting us from pathogens, goes deep into the organs each night to replenish them, triggered by the closing of our eyes. (Think of the times you have gone to bed early fretting about a problem, and woken in the morning with the solution.) Provided we are asleep before the gallbladder meridian "switches on," we benefit from this nightly renewal. If we stay awake beyond 11 P.M., we sometimes become conscious of its work and, as a result, we toss and turn, our minds going around and around.

The peak functioning time of the liver meridian is between 1 and 3 A.M. Night owls constantly challenge their ability to make plans, as well as their ability to make decisions. Some of the hardest patients to heal are the people who work on night shifts.

Taste

Each of the five elements has an associated taste. In Ilza Veith's translation of the *Nei Ching: Yellow Emperor's Classic of Internal Medicine*, we read that if people pay attention to and blend the five flavors well, then the benefits that ensue include straight bones, muscles that remain tender and young, breath and blood that

REMEMBER

If your color is green, you have a shouting or a whispering voice, you feel angry most of the time or never, and you smell rancid, then you have a Wood imbalance.

circulate freely, fine-textured pores, and, as a result, breath and bones filled with the essence of life.

The flavor that a person with a Wood Element imbalance will be drawn to is sour, such as lemons or vinegar. If you crave these things, you may be trying to correct the problem.

Controls

Anger locked into the body from inappropriate expression affects all the tendons and ligaments controlled by this element. The tension involved in controlling this emotion tunes the strings too tightly: look at the tight jaw, fists, and frown of an angry person, the deep grooves between the eyebrows. When the Wood Element is healthy and balanced we are supple and flexible in mind and body.

Body

The condition of the nails provides clues to the health of the Wood Element.

Weather

The wind has a strong effect on this element. Always wrap up well, especially around the neck area, if there is a cold wind. There is a point on the back of the neck called the wind pond. A draft here can trigger a cold. Air-conditioning can be damaging when it's directed onto the neck and shoulders. (Have a wrap or jacket with you in a restaurant in case you are seated in a draft from the air-conditioning unit.) Wind stirs up anger and can cause depression and instability. In the west of Wales, the name of a strong wind that blows there is the *vallen*, which is also the name for a depressive condition common in that region.

How to support the Wood Element
particularly for Enneagram types One, Eight, and Nine

• Get to bed in time to be asleep before 11 P.M.

• Pay attention to your intake of alcohol. Don't exceed safe limits.

• Avoid alcohol at lunchtime, when the liver is least able to detoxify the blood.

• Give up coffee. It is a toxin, even if it does taste delicious.

• Don't smoke cannabis. It is highly toxic to the liver, as are heroin and LSD.

• Eat more sour-tasting foods, such as vinegar and lemons – quince is particularly good. In addition, pay attention to exceptional cravings for these foods, which indicate that Wood is out of balance.

• Try, if you can, to eat only organically grown foods.

• Learn to express your anger in an appropriate fashion, and at the person who asked for it, at the time it is evoked. Don't let it fester. You will be surprised how well appropriate anger is accepted.

• Have a stack of old crockery ready to smash against a wall for those times when it is inappropriate to express anger openly.

• Take regular exercise to stretch and strengthen the tendons and ligaments, and disperse the tension caused by anger.

• Be mindful of how anger affects your body. Notice if you have clenched fists, a tight jaw, and so on.

• Take regular walks in the countryside or in the park.

• Change the background color on your computer to pale green, or take a break to look at trees or grass every now and again. (Tibetan monks use green paper to write on when they have eye strain.)

• Wear green if you suspect a Wood imbalance. If it is just not you, then wear green underwear.

• Protect your body, and especially your neck, from chill winds.

• Familiarize yourself with the pathways of the gallbladder and liver meridians, shown on page 79.

• Do the yoga exercises in Chapter Three suggested for the One, Eight, and Nine.

Visualization

This is a Buddhist meditation to elicit equanimity. It will help you deal with anger.

1 Sit in a comfortable position, ensuring that your spine is straight. If you sit in a chair, do not cross your legs, and make sure your feet are supported by the floor. If you are sitting cross-legged, you may find that your knees relax better toward the floor with a firm cushion or a foam block under your buttocks. A meditation cushion, or "zafu," is best, because you can slide to the front of it, which helps the knees go down and also helps keep the spine in the correct position (see the pictures on page 133).

2 Release any tension that you are holding in the body and rest one hand in the other, thumbs lightly touching. Take a couple of deep, relaxing breaths and then breathe quietly, not forcing it in. Your breathing will settle of its own accord. When your mind wanders, gently bring it home, back to the breath or the visualization. I like to use the image of a dog on an extending lead being brought gently back to base. If you scold your mind, it will be harder to let it settle again. All you need to do is repeatedly bring it home when it wanders and return to the task of attention.

3 Visualize someone for whom you have no feeling – such as a bus conductor, shop assistant, or stranger. Take some time to build up the picture of this person in your mind. Now visualize what they might do that would make you change your opinion of them positively – some kindly act, for example. Let the emotions arise and observe how your body reacts.

4 Now picture a dear friend, someone who is always kind and warm toward you. Let the warm feelings rise up and fill your body.

5 Next, picture something that person might do that would make you change your opinion. Stay with that image for a while.

6 Finally, picture someone you would consider to be an enemy. Let the feelings of anger arise. Now visualize them doing something that would change your opinion, which would make that person become "friend," and so dissolve your anger. Enjoy this feeling for a while. Note how what we feel depends largely on our own ego and projections.

7 When you are ready to come out of the visualization, take your attention back to your breath, make tiny movements with your fingers and toes to come back to your body, and slowly open your eyes when you feel able.

Season
Summer

Emotion
Joy

Meridians
Heart, Small intestine, Pericardium, Three heater

Color
Red

Sound
Laughing

Odor
Scorched

Time of day
11 A.M.–3 P.M. (heart and small intestine)
7 P.M.–11 P.M. (pericardium and three heater)

Taste
Bitter

Controls
Circulation

Body
Complexion

Weather
Heat

Season

Have you ever lighted a fire and not known people to gather around it, attracted by its warmth and the lively flickering of the flames? We cannot resist the pheromone of fire. The Fire Element functions at its peak in summer, when we are surrounded in nature by the growth of the seeds we planted in spring, luxuriating in warmth and long hours of light. The borders fill out, and we can exercise a true generosity of spirit, sharing abundance, be it armfuls of fruit and vegetables, or a bunch of sweetly scented roses. With the Fire Element in balance there is a natural expression of joy and warmth toward fellow human beings, particularly in summer, but generally in life. In summer we have extra energy to spend time socializing, and to take time out with our families and friends. There is ebullience, an enthusiasm, and an opening of the heart chakra.

At this point I want to introduce you to a fundamental law of the five elements – the Law of Mother/Child: as with the Enneagram there is a movement of energy in this system, too. All Elements are interconnected. When one meridian is out of balance there is a side effect. We receive abundant rewards in summer if the mother element, Wood, was honored in spring, fueling the energy of Fire – but what if we failed to turn the soil and plant seeds in

spring? This is why it is most important to live in a way that supports all five elements.

If you come alive only in summer, this is an indication of a Fire imbalance, as much as disliking summer is.

Emotion

There are four meridians in the Fire Element: heart, small intestine, pericardium, and the three heater (sometimes called the triple burner). Each has a strong effect on the emotion, joy, and how it is expressed in relationships – be it in close relationship or in the wider world. Think about the nature of fire: blazing flames spreading sparks up high, tiny flickers, raging infernos, slow burning. Look for how the emotion manifests in people with a Fire imbalance.

We all know the stereotype of the tragic comic, fooling around making us laugh, while all the time sad at heart. I have regularly observed this element to be out of balance in the types of the emotional/feeling triad of the Enneagram Twos, Threes, and Fours. Not that a Fire imbalance isn't sometimes an issue with other types (always bear in mind the interconnections); it is just that it seems to be commonly out of balance in this triad: the Threes seeking love and approval through what they do, the Twos serving others' needs for love, and the Fours in search of their missing love.

Meridians – heart and small intestine

The heart meridian is the supreme controller of the body, the king, ruler of the palace. People with a primary imbalance in the heart meridian have a strong presence, just like royalty. When they walk into a room we notice them – we notice them even when they stand still, quietly doing nothing at all. They are the directors, head teachers, politicians, and leaders. Although they may have big hearts, they often don't take the time to check in with their emotions. Driven people, they often find it hard to honor their hearts by spending time giving love to, and receiving love from, their close ones, to the physical detriment of their hearts. Almost without exception I found this particular Fire imbalance in my Enneagram type Three patients. And it is often not until their first heart attack that Threes stop to examine their lives. It is literally a matter of life and death that Threes learn how they can support this element and acknowledge their emotions and give their hearts due rest.

The small intestine meridian, paired with the heart, and running close by it, but up the outside of the arm and over the shoulder to the ear, is the official of discrimination. On a physical level, the small intestine absorbs what is nutritious for the body and throws out the rubbish. The small intestine meridian helps us on a psychological level to discriminate what is good for us and what is bad, particularly when it comes to our relationships. We probably all can name a friend who makes us cringe as they are, once again, drawn toward the worst possible relationship, the wrong job, the house built on sand … you know the pattern. Look for this imbalance in Twos and Fours, especially.

Meridians – pericardium and three heater

On a physical level the pericardium sheathes the heart to protect it. On a psychological level the pericardium meridian, also known as the heart protector, is like the secretary in the outer office, preventing anyone from walking in on you without an appointment. The heart is our most precious organ. Not to be given away lightly to all and sundry, it needs protection. When a type Two,

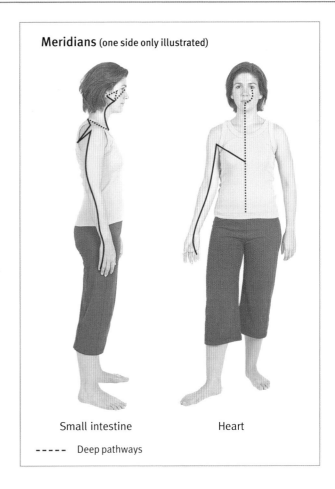

Meridians (one side only illustrated)

Small intestine   Heart

- - - - -   Deep pathways

desperate to be needed, works too hard at friendship, trying to create/maintain too many close relationships, it puts a strain on the pericardium. What's the point in having a secretary if you ignore him or her? These are the people who wear their hearts on their sleeves, who are all heart. There is a pericardium point on the inner wrist called Great Mound. I think of this meridian as providing a mound to hide behind when too many people demand a piece of you.

The three heater is related to a function rather than an organ – controlling heat and cold, making sure that all the organs are kept at their optimum operating temperature. On a psychological level, like all the Fire Element meridians, it affects relationships, but this time, it is associated with wider relationships, those with colleagues and acquaintances, and our constancy in close relationships. When a friend blows hot and cold

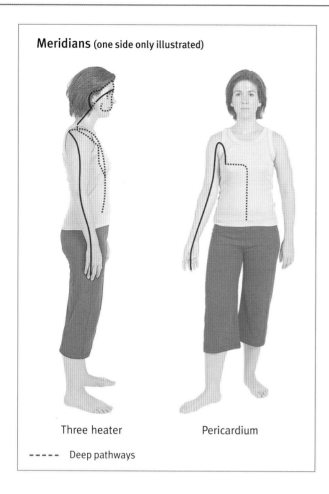

Meridians (one side only illustrated)

Three heater   Pericardium

----- Deep pathways

Color

This shows as red, or a lack of red.

Sound

The sound connected with the Fire Element is laughing. Whatever the person says there is a kind of lilt of laughter in the voice, and often whatever they are saying is actually accompanied by laughter. This gets more extreme when there is an imbalance. (I wish I had a coin for every time I have heard a person with a Fire Element imbalance laughingly describe to me some devastating event in their life.) Conversely, there may be an inability to laugh. (My charismatic teacher, J. R. Worsley, used to crawl under the treatment couch on all fours and pop up the other side to take a patient's pulse, just to test a sad person's ability to laugh.)

Odor

The odor of a Fire Element imbalance is scorched – a bit like the smell of freshly ironed laundry. Next time an over-the-top, laughing, gushing type Two flings themselves into your arms, take note of their odor.

Time of day

Peak functioning time for the heart is between 11 A.M. and 1 P.M., with a corresponding low 12 hours later. It is common for heart attacks to occur at night, during this low. Though Threes might scoff, pleading lack of time, it does the heart enormous good to rest for half an hour or so with an after-lunch nap.

The small intestine meridian has its peak functioning time between 1 P.M. and 3 P.M. This is a time when we are most able to discriminate, a perfect time for editing and for other activities that require discrimination.

The pericardium's peak functioning time is between 7 P.M. and 9 P.M. This is a good time for socializing, relaxing and laughing with friends – around a fire in winter, or outside in the evening sunshine in summer.

The three heater's peak functioning time is between 9 P.M. and 11 P.M. Time to cozy up and get ready for bed. In our modern world, with electric light and televisions, this meridian is constantly being challenged.

with you, it may well be that their three heater is out of balance. One day you call and they can't get enough of you; another, you get a cold draft and wonder, "What did I say wrong?" I have seen this meridian affected when Twos build resentment, and it is very common in Fours when they get into the push/pull behavior. This meridian can also be damaged by having a parent or a lover who blows hot and cold with you.

An imbalance of the three heater can affect our ability to feel comfortable one-to-one or in a group. We should be able to move smoothly between either, not favoring one over another.

Fire Element people sometimes have a problem with touch. They may seek an inordinate amount of touch, or they may freeze when you move too close. Massage is a good way to stimulate all the elements, but it is particularly effective for Fire imbalances.

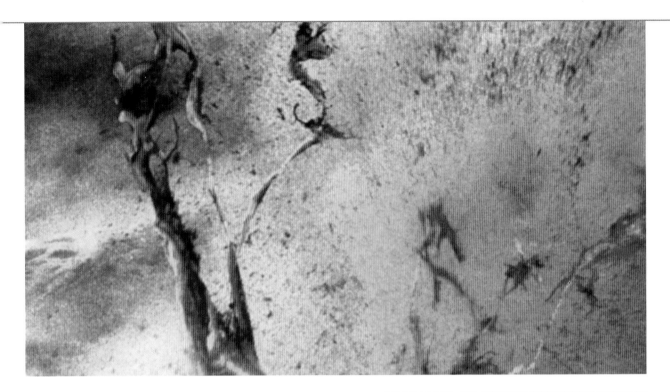

Taste

The flavor associated with the Fire Element is bitter. Strong-flavored green vegetables – endive, chicory cabbage – and beer all stimulate the Fire Element. Pay attention if you are craving this taste, or if you are averse to it, as you may need to look at the Fire Element.

Controls

All matters relating to circulation are linked to this element. The three heater works to maintain optimum thermostatic conditions for the body to function under, so that all the organs work efficiently. The heart pumps the blood. The small intestine absorbs what nourishes us from the blood and cleanses it, and the pericardium sheathes and protects the heart. Circulation problems, such as varicose veins, high blood pressure, and blood clots, are strongly influenced by how well we honor our Fire Element.

Body

The complexion of a person shows the health of the Fire Element. People with an imbalance in any Fire Meridian often have heart problems and trouble with their veins and arteries generally. If the three heater is implicated, they may have hot flushes, be constantly chilly, or veer wildly from one extreme to the other, or one area of the body may be excessively cold or hot.

If this describes you, lie down naked, and feel your torso on the lower abdomen, just above the belly button, and on your chest. If these areas are not equally warm, there is an imbalance in your three heater.

Weather

Heat affects the Fire Element. Sunbathing at noon, for example, covering up inadequately in cold weather, and taking scalding hot baths and saunas can all have a detrimental effect on this element.

REMEMBER

If you have a laughing/lack of laughing voice, red/lack of red around the mouth and eyes, smell scorched, and feel overly joyful/sad, you have a Fire Element imbalance.

How to support the Fire Element
particularly for Enneagram types Two and Three (and some Fours)

- Take a nap after lunch for half an hour.
- Make time to socialize with friends, particularly in summer. In winter socialize around a fire.
- Eat plenty of leafy green vegetables.
- Go to bed between 9 P.M. and 11 P.M.
- Book a regular massage.
- Take long, comfortably warm baths, surrounded by candles.
- Make time for candlelit dinners with your partner.
- Get help with sensate focus exercises if you have a problem with touch.
- Be your own secretary in the outer office – learn to say, "No, you can't come in right now."
- Be sensible about sunbathing. Stay indoors at noon, or sit in a café in the shade.
- Give up coffee; it's toxic and it makes the heart race. And though it is bitter, it is not a healthful way to get this taste.
- Take a glass of wine with your meal in the evenings, unless you have a problem with alcohol.
- Do not exceed safe limits with alcohol and never take cocaine or Ecstasy – as well as illegal, they are high risk for people with a Fire Element imbalance.
- Don't imbibe Fire by smoking.
- Learn to recognize when your flames are burning too hot, or are barely flickering.
- Wear red, if your Fire feels low. If it is not your color, then wear red underwear.
- Note the love that you receive.
- Familiarize yourself with the pathways of the heart, small intestine, pericardium, and three heater meridians on pages 85 and 86.
- Do the yoga postures for Twos, Threes, and Fours on pages 110–15.

Visualization

1 Sit in a comfortable position, ensuring that your spine is straight. If you sit in a chair, do not cross your legs, and make sure your feet are supported by the floor. If you are sitting cross-legged, you may find that your knees relax better toward the floor with a firm cushion or a foam block under your buttocks. A meditation cushion, or "zafu," is best, because you can slide to the front of it, which helps the knees go down and also helps keep the spine in the correct position (see the pictures on page 133).

2 Breathe quietly, not forcing the breath, simply following the flow with your mind.

3 Picture a person whom you love sitting in front of you. Look closely at every detail of the face, particularly the eyes.

4 Let love for this person swell in your heart, and let the feeling grow.

5 When the feeling is strong, extend the love out to other people you are close to, picturing each one as you do.

6 Feel love pouring out of you like a stream of nectar to these beloved people.

7 Now feel love surrounding and returning to you, and bask in the glow of love given and love received. Imagine an aura of pale green light.

8 Extend this light beyond your body, out into the universe.

9 When you are ready, come back to the breath, make tiny movements with your fingers and toes, and slowly open your eyes when you feel able.

the earth element

Season

The Chinese have an extra season: late summer. One way to recognize it is that it has a flavor of all the other seasons. You step outside one morning, and it's misty with a winter chill; the next day it is baking hot, like high summer. Another day you notice a leaf starting to turn; another it feels fresh and spring-like. This is harvest time – the gathering in of the fruits of your labor. Gardens in late summer produce a cornucopia of fruit and vegetables. Blink twice and a baby zucchini turns into a huge gourd. This is also when seeds ripen and set for the coming year.

The person who made plans and decisions during spring, who enjoyed the laughter and fun of summer, now gathers in this harvest. You may feel significantly better in this late summer season if you have an Earth imbalance when the element gets a little more energy, but if it already has too much, you may feel worse.

The Earth Element is our grounding, our foundation: the hot ash of fire transformed. Picture the earth, our home, ablaze to the point of liquid in the center, cool and fruitful on the outside, supporting life. Earth people, when balanced, are strong, grounded, stable, nurturing, and motherly. But if life has not fed them, if they were inappropriately mothered in childhood, or if they neglect/abuse the nourishment they give their bodies, then the Earth Element destabilizes, like crumbling soil. As a result, they become anxious, constantly worrying, churning things over and over. Think of the nature of soil: soggy, unstable, parched, fertile – the character of any of these could be reflected in the Earth person.

Emotion

The emotion controlled by the Earth Element is sympathy and also worry. Think of motherly nurturing energy. The appropriate expression of this emotion enables us to feel empathy for our fellow human beings – an overdose generates the cloying "Jewish mother" stereotype.

When poor diet or inadequate emotional nurturing stresses the Earth Element, sympathy is affected. We all need to give and take, in more or less equal quantities, accepting that occasionally the balance tilts more one way than the other. Problems arise only when the tilt is consistently more in one direction than it is in the other.

When a person is stuck in sympathy, it can transmute into martyrdom. "I've worked my fingers to the bone for you and you never think about me." (Remember the children's story of the Little Red Hen and the wheat she planted, cut, and made into bread for her chicks?)

Too much giving and nurturing exhausts the Earth Element and often translates into a problem with digestion and a mind wracked with constant anxiety. Conversely, a person may be of the opposite extreme and be unable to recognize need in others and so be totally unsympathetic.

Meridians – stomach and spleen

The stomach meridian, associated with digestion, the so-called rotting and ripening of food, is also linked to our ability to rot and ripen mentally. We all need to be able to take things in, to assimilate information and ideas – to compost them, if you will. But a compost heap needs to be left to settle after churning. With imbalanced Earth, the person may constantly churn things over (much as a Nine does, failing to get into action), exhausting him- or herself in the process. They often have faces wracked with worry, foreheads creased with lines, and the centers of their eyebrows raised and pinched together. This can be a soft, puppy-dog look, with a head tilted to one side, as they listen sympathetically. We need equality of nurture: Twos, take note.

The spleen, apart from its role in regenerating cells and storing blood, is the transport official, responsible for delivering nourishment to all parts of the body. When it's weak, our ability to think straight is affected, and we become fuzzy and unclear. The spleen has the ability to support organs, and it is not unusual to see difficulties with prolapses (hemorrhoids, for example) when this meridian is weak.

Color

Appropriately, the color of the Earth Element is yellow, like the golden fields of late summer waiting for harvest. Look for yellow around the mouth and eyes of a person with an Earth imbalance.

Sound

The tone of voice of a person with an Earth imbalance is singing. Listen to your voice-mail messages to hear it. When you hear a voice going up and down in a singsong fashion, like someone crooning to a baby, this is the Earth Element speaking out, and it is heard in men just

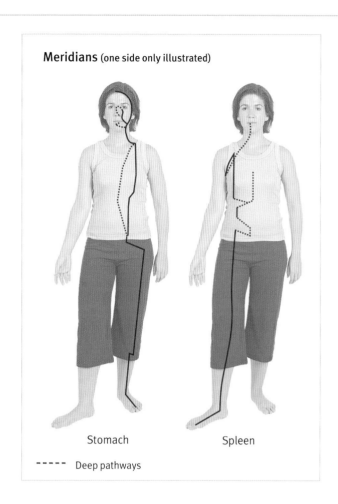

Meridians (one side only illustrated)

Stomach   Spleen

- - - - - Deep pathways

as often as it is in women. Or you might identify the flat monotone of the "lack of" singing voice.

Odor

The odor associated with an Earth imbalance is fragrant. Next time someone is being saccharine sweet to you, and you feel smothered, have a surreptitious sniff and see what you think.

Time of day

The stomach meridian has peak energy between 7 A.M. and 9 A.M. – yet when do we have our main meal of the day in the West? Eat a good breakfast and the stomach meridian will have enough strength to digest almost anything and to perform its physical and psychological functions well. The old adage of "eat like a king at breakfast, a prince at midday, and a pauper at tea time" holds true. The very worst thing you can do to the Earth Element is to skip breakfast, starve all day, and have a good blow-out meal at night. When we eat a main meal in the evening there it sits, inadequately digested, in the poor old stomach, which is forced to work when it should be resting. Sometimes, weight problems can be resolved by changing your eating habits to fit in with the schedule of the stomach. When I studied in Guangzhou, in Canton, China, I used to take great delight watching local students at the college downing enormous bowls of steaming vegetables, noodles, or rice with a little meat or tofu at breakfast.

If we have had a good breakfast between 7 A.M. and 9 A.M., when the spleen kicks in between 9 A.M. and 11 A.M. getting things moving, we have plenty of energy and a clear head for work. It gets us moving into action – a common Nine problem.

Taste

With an imbalance in the Earth Element we may eat excessively, trying to obtain nourishment, but we are attracted to all the wrong types of foods, particularly the sweet flavor (which is the first taste we have in our mother's milk). Sweets, cakes, bread, dairy foods, milk chocolate – foods that are best taken in moderation – are often eaten in excess. The body can be large and bloated, or cavernous and malnourished looking. At the other extreme, there may be little or no appetite, no enthusiasm, for food or for life. I have seen quite a few Twos with an imbalance in Earth, obsessively giving, but inside craving to receive, and in many Nines, who tend to blow out on sweet foods and by generally overeating.

> **REMEMBER**
>
> If you are yellow around the eyes and mouth, have a singing/monotone voice, smell fragrant, and have issues around sympathy, you have an Earth imbalance.

Controls

The Earth Element controls digestion and assimilation within the body.

Body

The muscles and flesh are associated with the Earth Element. The muscle tone of a person can tell you a lot about the state of this element. Are they soggy Earth – waterlogged, with heavy ankles, and carrying a lot of excess fluid – or are they parched and impoverished Earth? The mouth is also associated with the Earth Element, and this can give you more clues.

Weather

Humidity is the weather associated with the Earth Element. It can trigger the typical headache common to an Earth imbalance that is hard to locate, but sometimes throbs high on either side of the forehead and is accompanied by nausea. A humid climate can make us feel heavy and wilted.

How to support the Earth Element
particularly for Enneagram types Two and Nine

- Always have breakfast, but finish eating before 9 A.M.
- Try to avoid eating a heavy meal later than 6 P.M. Lunchtime is the best time.
- Watch your intake of sugary, sweet things.
- Take regular exercise to tone your muscles.
- Eat at a table, without a radio, television, or newspapers.
- Eat regular meals.
- Allow enough time to digest your food properly after a meal.
- Avoid eating too many cold foods, as it damages the spleen.
- Chew your food properly.
- Don't eat food on the run.
- Don't have a yo-yo diet, veering wildly between starvation and overeating.
- Always leave the table after a meal thinking you could eat a little bit more.
- Learn to say no, to recognize that you don't always have to leap in with caring behavior.
- Ask for help when you need it. Let others have the satisfaction of nurturing you.
- Get your hands in the earth literally, gardening, digging, sowing, and planting.
- Wear yellow to support the Earth Element.
- Walk barefoot on the grass.
- Lie flat out on the ground and feel the supporting earth. (The last three I recommend particularly after being in a plane.)
- Avoid too much humidity at home, where you can control your environment. Use a dehumidifier if necessary.
- Familiarize yourself with the pathways of the stomach and spleen meridians, shown on page 91.
- Do the Sun Sequence on pages 124–25.

Visualization

1 Sit in a comfortable position, ensuring that your spine is straight. If you sit in a chair, do not cross your legs, and make sure your feet are supported by the floor. If you are sitting cross-legged, you may find that your knees relax better toward the floor with a firm cushion or a foam block under your buttocks. A meditation cushion, or "zafu," is best, because you can slide to the front of it, which helps the knees go down and also helps keep the spine in the correct position (see the pictures on page 133).

2 Picture yourself standing by a beautiful field full of ripening wheat, in the golden light of early evening.

3 As you walk slowly to the center of the field, you feel the wheat brushing against your hands and against your legs.

4 In the center of the field you find a clearing with warm russet earth.

5 There on the earth you find an object that represents what nurtures you in life.

6 Walk around the object, taking in every detail of it, and then pick it up or stretch out a hand and touch it.

7 Take time to absorb the meaning and the energy of the object.

8 Put down the object and thank Mother Earth for giving you insight into what nurtures you.

9 Retrace your steps back to the outside of the golden wheat field, knowing that at any time in the future when you feel you need to, you can return to find guidance about what will nurture you appropriately.

10 When you are ready, come back to the breath, make tiny movements with your fingers and toes, and slowly open your eyes when you feel able.

the metal element

Season
Autumn

Emotion
Grief

Meridians
Lung and colon

Color
White

Sound
Weeping

Odor
Rotten

Time of day
3 A.M.–7 A.M.

Taste
Pungent

Controls
Elimination

Body
Body hair, skin

Weather
Dryness

Season

Leaves turn and there is a magnificent blaze of color when autumn, like a dying swan, folds her wings on the year. This is the season when the Metal Element flourishes. When it is balanced, we look around us at the splendor and our spirits lift; we feel closer to the Divine. Next, when the leaves fall they give us a broader view through the skeleton of branches. As without, so within: the body/mind/spirit sees beyond the superficial at this time. Whatever form our connection with the spirit takes, we all need this dimension, be it with God, Allah, Buddha, Christ – or simply by opening our hearts when we gaze at the blaze of leaves.

However, if you have an imbalance in Metal you may dislike the poignancy of autumn, or feel good only at this time.

Emotion

The Metal Element enables us to express grief appropriately, at the time of loss, and then to let go and move on. Autumn is when we shed regrets and resentments, which are also forms of grief. When autumn storms rip through the branches, shaking off dead wood – so should we. We can use the energy of Metal to clear out musty cupboards and, as we do, we should think of doing the same at a deeper level. If the broader view is bleak, look at what attachments are not serving you well. What/who can you do without?

This element is connected with the father energy: your earthly father, and also the heavenly father. Earth Element people have problems, or an exceptional closeness, with their mothers; with Metal, it is fathers. They often report having tyrannical fathers, resulting in a crushing lack of confidence.

The Metal Element is named for the precious materials in the rocks: gold and silver, gems and crystals. It relates to the quality that we experience in our lives. You often see Metal Element people wearing a beautiful jewel, or something unique or striking, in an attempt to counter a lack of self-worth – and yes, you are right, this does relate strongly to Enneagram type Four. I found that patients with a Metal Element imbalance, almost without exception, were Fours. Treatments on the colon and lung meridians had a significant beneficial effect, dispelling feelings of loss, abandonment, and low self-esteem, helping them to regain confidence. I also identified Enneagram type Five patients with this imbalance, and occasionally Ones, though it was not primary.

Meridians – colon and lung

The meridians of the Metal Element are in charge of elimination. The colon is the official in charge of getting rid of our rubbish – physically by eliminating feces; psychologically by ridding us of regrets and resentments. The colon meridian passes

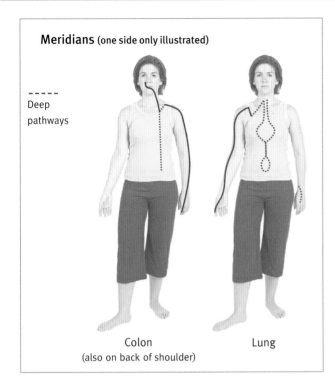

Meridians (one side only illustrated)

- - - - -
Deep
pathways

Colon
(also on back of shoulder)

Lung

over the shoulders, an area where we hold resentment and grief. (Look at the posture of a deeply resentful or grief-stuck person.) If you have shoulder pain, think about what negativity you are holding on to.

The lung meridian is paired with the colon. The lungs, too, are responsible for elimination in the process of expiration. In every breath we release we are expelling toxins. But think about the word "inspiration" – does it not accurately describe that connection with the Divine that is the blessing of the Metal Element? You could say it is in charge of quality control. The vital Chi is our gift from heaven, taken in by the lungs. Ask yourself: are you dancing with the rhythm of life, and feeding your Metal Element?

The posture recommended for Fours on pages 114–15 frees up the shoulders and opens the chest, giving space to the lungs working physically and emotionally on the Metal Element.

Color
The color associated with a Metal imbalance is white. Though it is now fashionable in the Far East to have Western-style white weddings, this is the color they traditionally associate with grief, and certainly in China, the bride would have worn the more lucky color, red. Look for white on the face of the newly bereaved, or an asthmatic, or someone with bowel problems.

Sound
This is weeping, perhaps the easiest of the five sounds to identify. No matter what the person says there is a scratchy tone, rather high, that sounds as if the person is just about to burst into tears.

Odor
It is appropriate that the odor associated with Metal is rotten. Walk in the woods in autumn to catch the mushroomy, overripe smell of Metal.

Time of day
Have you ever been woken up at some ungodly hour by the need to rush to the bathroom? The colon meridian has a peak of energy between 5 A.M. and 7 A.M. and, inconvenient though you may find this when your child wakes you at dawn, it is the most effective time for us to void our bowels. Acknowledging this fact, and getting going a little earlier in the day, has been known to cure constipation.

The lung meridian precedes the bowel, with a peak of energy between 3 A.M. and 5 A.M. Although the lungs are greatly restored by sleep during this time, it is also a potent time for connecting with Spirit. This may explain why monks and nuns rise in the early hours to meditate or pray.

Taste
The pungent taste of onions, garlic, and spices is associated with Metal. If you have a craving for curry, it may be that you are trying to feed this element. An aversion to these foods can also indicate an imbalance.

Controls
The Metal Element, with the colon and lung meridians, controls elimination, as described above. The posture

for type Ones, shown on pages 108–9, is also beneficial in helping to counter constipation.

Body

The Metal Element is associated with body hair and with the nose. The skin also breathes, and we can read much about the state of the Metal Element in people by the state of their skin.

Weather

A dry climate has a detrimental effect on the Metal Element. The lungs are nurtured by there being a reasonable amount of moisture in the air, and a cough, or other lung problems, may result from breathing air that is overly dry.

REMEMBER

If you are white around the eyes and mouth, have a weeping tone of voice, are dogged by grief and regrets, and smell rotten, you have a Metal imbalance.

Diaphragmatic breathing exercise and visualization

1 Lie flat on a mat on the floor, with a straight spine, the back of your neck lengthened, and any tight clothing around the waist or chest loosened. (Ladies, it helps to undo your bra.) Lightly rest your hands on your abdomen, with your middle fingers just touching. Unclench your jaw. Feel your face soften, like melting wax.

2 Take your attention to the breath. Filling your lungs, inhale deeply and slowly (as if pouring water down into a bottle), and feel your abdomen expand as your diaphragm goes down. Next, exhale slowly, feeling your diaphragm relax up toward the heart, and your tummy flatten. Picture the diaphragm as you breathe.

3 Continue this deep breathing. Count to six as you breathe in, hold for six counts, breathe out to a count of six, and hold the breath out for a count of six. (You can adjust the counts to suit yourself if you find this is too long.)

4 Keep this even breathing rhythm going for 5–10 minutes, until you feel very relaxed.

5 Then, breathing normally and quietly without counting, feel your body lighten, as if you are floating on a cloud.

6 Imagine yourself surrounded by clear white light that brightens with every breath.

7 Picture yourself breathing in this light, so that it surrounds and penetrates every cell of your body, healing and replenishing.

8 Now imagine that this light is emanating from you, and connecting you with the universe, and bask in the sensation.

9 When you are ready to finish, bring your attention back to the breath.

10 Bring your attention back to your body, making tiny movements with your fingers and toes. Bend up your knees and rock slightly from side to side, and when you are ready to sit up, roll over onto your right side and use your arms to help yourself up.

How to support the Metal Element
particularly for Enneagram types Four (and also some Fives and Ones)

- Get up before 7 A.M. to aid elimination.
- Perform breathing exercises (see opposite).
- Find a way that connects you to Spirit, and make time for this.
- Do exercises that open the chest and lungs, such as running or swimming.
- Eat more, or less, pungent foods, depending on the state of Metal in you.
- If you smoke – stop!
- Learn to recognize your unique qualities, and to appreciate them.
- Have a good cleansing, on all levels, in autumn.
- Eating watermelon, or other types of melon, helps cure constipation.
- Find ways to "father" yourself, if this was lacking in your life.
- Practice giving yourself consideration.
- Remember that the qualities you most admire in others are yours, too.
- Put aside an area in your home that connects you with Spirit. Place things there that connect you with Spirit.
- Listen to music that you find uplifting.
- Yoga and meditation are particularly helpful to the Metal Element.
- Learn the pathways of the colon and lung meridians, illustrated on page 97.
- Do the yoga posture regularly on pages 114–15 for type Fours.
- Do the yoga posture for type Ones on pages 108–9 if you need to speed up elimination of waste from the body.
- Whenever you hear the tone of a cell phone, let it remind you to take a deep breath.

the water element

Season

Today, with rain pouring down after weeks of drought, I am reminded of the Water Element, which has its peak of energy in the winter. We may complain about the rain, especially when it's constant, but you only have to watch people in the parched countries of Africa, celebrating its arrival, to be reminded of its importance to our lives.

The Chinese say that in winter we should stay indoors "like an old pickle jar in the basement." This is the season when we should restore our energy by being quieter, wrapping up warmly and having long sleeps at night. It is absolutely fine to get up at 5 A.M. in summer, when we have an abundance of energy, but ideally we should not rise before dawn in winter. Modern lifestyles often do not permit this, and our bodies pay the price with exhaustion. However, we need to do what we can toward making winter a restorative time, in order to fill our reservoirs for the growth in spring. Our seeds need to rest, tucked up under the soil.

Emotion

The emotion controlled by the Water Element is fear. When our Water Element is honored we are able to express fear appropriately. When we do not give this element the adequate rest it desires, fear gets out of control. We all know people whose first response to anything is fearful, doubting, and we can probably name friends who are fearless to the point of self-neglect. Both indicate an imbalance in the Water Element. The three Enneagram types that relate to fear – the Fives, Sixes, and Sevens – almost always have an imbalance in this element.

Meridians – bladder and kidneys

China is famed for its control of water. Huge importance is placed on irrigation projects: dams, directing water to the rice terraces and controlling its retention, lakes and rivers. The bladder and kidney meridians are our water board officials. They are responsible for making sure that the 80 percent water of which we are made is distributed properly. Bladder and kidney meridians control glandular function, the synovial fluid in the joints, and the constant purification processes of urination and sweating.

Water is the great shape-shifter of the elements. Think of its forms: steam, ice, droplets, oceans, rivers, clouds. So powerful it can grind down a mountain or create the Grand Canyon. It is a key element in shaping our earth. Water makes our planet an object of wonder to view from space – and without it none of us would survive. Water Element people can have this strength; but if the bladder and kidney meridians are not honored with adequate rest, the body pays the price with exhaustion and excessive fear.

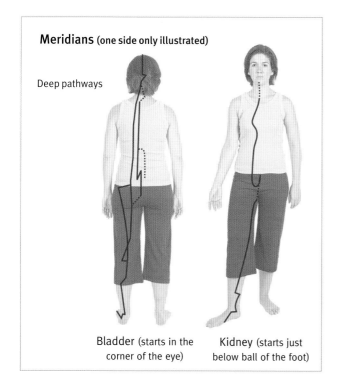

Meridians (one side only illustrated)

Deep pathways

Bladder (starts in the corner of the eye)

Kidney (starts just below ball of the foot)

Time of day

The bladder meridian has its peak energy between 3 P.M. and 5 P.M. The kidneys have a peak of energy between 5 P.M. and 7 P.M. – a time when many people go into a slump. Working into this time does not help the kidneys.

Taste

People with an imbalance in the Water Element crave, or have a strong dislike of, salty food.

Controls

The bones and marrow are controlled by Water. The structure of a person is, therefore, strongly related to this element. Look how a life lived in fear affects a body. The knees and back become weak if Water is compromised, and in Chinese medical law the brain is considered to be marrow – often reflected in confused thinking when there are bladder or kidney complaints in older people.

Body

You can tell a lot about the state of the Water Element in people by the condition of their back – by their posture. Because this element controls the bones, the spine is commonly affected. The bladder meridian, the longest in the body, travels down the back on either side of the spine, from the corner of the eyes over the top of the head, right down the back to the little toe. Familiarize yourself with this and the kidney meridian shown at left.

The kidney rules the head hair. Only the very old in China allow themselves to go gray, which is like carrying a banner saying. "Look how much sex I've had!" It is common to see thinning hair in people of both sexes where there is a kidney imbalance. A good thick head of hair usually indicates strong kidneys.

The Water Element also has a connection with the ears and hearing. Remember that deafness type Sixes are prone to when they are in a state of panic?

Weather

Was it Oscar Wilde who said that there was no such thing as bad weather – there was only inadequate

Bones and glands suffer, and back pain and weak knees are common problems. One way to make people pay attention to the kidney meridian is to tell them it is responsible for their sexual energy.

We all need to recognize that coffee and tea are diuretics – they are like undrinking. Coffee is a diuretic because it's an irritant to the kidneys, and toxic to the liver. Is it any wonder the number of people who complain they have lost interest in sex?

Color

This shows as blue or blue-black.

Sound

A clear indicator of an imbalance in the Water Element is a groaning tone to the voice. I call it a "deep down in the boots" tone.

Odor

The Water Element odor is putrid. The best way to experience it (and apologies for the suggestion) is to smell one of those stairwells drunks use as a toilet.

clothing? Our mothers were right, we do need to wrap up well in cold weather! You'd think that this goes without saying, but once again modern life intervenes. With stores air-conditioned like freezers in high summer, it is not only in winter we need to pay attention.

The current fashion for bare midriffs, no matter what the weather, is storing up kidney trouble for the future. My first-ever patient was a truck driver with arthritis in his elbow. It didn't take long to figure out that his habit of driving with his elbow sticking out the open window was the cause of his problem. An osteopath once told me you can x-ray anyone over the age of 30 and see signs of

REMEMBER

If you are blue around the mouth and eyes, have a groaning voice, smell putrid, and have issues with fear, you have a Water Element imbalance.

arthritis, which may explain why it is such a common diagnosis, but not one to buy into necessarily. My patient made some changes and never suffered again.

Visualization

1 Sit in a comfortable position, ensuring that your spine is straight. If you sit in a chair, do not cross your legs, and make sure your feet are supported by the floor. If you are sitting cross-legged, you may find that your knees relax better toward the floor with a firm cushion or a foam block under your buttocks. A meditation cushion, or "zafu," is best, because you can slide to the front of it, which helps the knees go down and also helps keep the spine in the correct position (see the pictures on page 133).

2 Picture yourself sitting on a beach in warm sunshine, in the golden early evening light of a setting sun, by the water's edge with your back up against a large rock.

3 Notice that as the waves move, they pause for a moment at each end of the turn.

4 Now breathe, timing your breath with the movements of the waves. Breathe in for a few counts, pause, breathe out for a few counts, pause. (Choose a count to suit you.) Keep this rhythm going for a few minutes.

5 Now let go of the count, and just focus on the natural rhythm of your breath.

6 Feel the strength of the rock behind you, immovable despite the buffeting of water over eons.

7 Think of the plant and animal life that this strong rock supports, of the fluidity of the water around it.

8 Become that steady rock and feel these qualities.

9 When you feel strong enough, take your attention back to the breath, listen to the sounds around you, make tiny movements with your fingers and toes, and finally open your eyes slowly.

How to support the water element
particularly for Enneagram types Five, Six, and Seven

- Get adequate sleep/rest in winter.
- Take care not to overwork. Stop work at 5 P.M. if possible.
- Keep your kidneys well covered in cold weather, and stay out of drafts.
- Drink sufficient water – at least 3 pints (1.5 liters) a day.
- Cut back on drinking tea.
- Give up drinking coffee.
- Cover up well generally in cold weather.
- A nap after lunch helps the Water Element.
- Watch your intake of salty foods.
- If you cycle in winter, don't wear shorts. Even if you get hot, you must keep your knees and the small of your back covered.
- Regularly massage your kidneys with your fists (they lie under the bottom ribs on your back) on either side of the spine. Do it until you feel the warmth.
- Avoid too much sex. (If you are exhausted afterward, that's too much!)
- Socialize in winter in quieter ways, around a fire, dining with friends, and so on.
- Learn to recognize the signs of exhaustion before illness intervenes.
- Familiarize yourself with the pathways of the bladder and kidney meridians, shown on page 101.
- Do the yoga postures recommended for Fives, Sixes, and Sevens on pages 116–21, and for the first chakra on pages 130–33.

CHAPTER THREE

The postures

Living in the mind only
is like living in a virtual world
It may be your personal reality,
but that personal reality
is still an illusion.

Roy Whenary   *The Texture of Being*

introduction to the postures

There is information about yoga postures contained in this chapter that you are not likely to come across anywhere else. However, it is always best to learn yoga under the guidance of a properly qualified yoga teacher if you possibly can. But if you are following the postures from a book, ask a friend to read out the instructions to you and to watch and make sure that you are carrying them out correctly. Any good yoga class will include the postures in this book, or ones that are very similar. When it comes to doing the posture for your own type, you can silently repeat the affirmation and visualize all the benefits that I describe.

I have chosen postures that are beneficial for each type, but I don't wish to imply that they are suitable *only* for that type. Yogis say you are as young as your spine, and for the spine to achieve maximum flexibility a practice should, therefore, contain a posture that flexes the spine forward, bends it backward, rotates it, and flexes it sideways. You can use postures for any type to devise a balanced practice, but prioritize the posture for your own type and do it regularly.

Warm up before your practice, limber each joint from the toes up, and get your circulation going generally. Don't worry about any clicking or cracking; people think this is crunching bone, but it is just the fluid in the joints "popping" as it becomes more viscous. Check with your doctor if you have a medical condition that might affect your yoga practice. And never take your head below your heart in postures if you have high blood pressure.

Remember to counterpose a posture that takes the spine in only one direction – see the posture for type Five on pages 116–17, which arches the back and is counterposed with a posture that curls the spine forward.

Yoga is a science. It works on the internal organs as well as on the musculature. People often ask, "Why does yoga make you bend in all those peculiar positions?" The answer is that apart from the flexibility all that stretching promotes, the internal organs also get a workout. First they are compressed and then, when they are released, they receive an inrush of freshly oxygenated blood.

I cannot emphasize enough the importance of correct breathing while doing the postures. When you first start this is difficult, and I don't want you to worry about it … take an extra breath whenever you need to. In time, correct breathing will become second nature. It is natural to breathe in deeply with an opening movement, when the arms lift, for example, and to breathe out with a closing/folding movement. The breathing mostly follows this rule, so if you are in any doubt, follow it.

The greatest benefit comes from doing regular yoga practice. This requires a degree of dedication, but bear in mind that you will get out of your practice exactly what you put in. Find a space where you are relaxed, comfortable, warm, and will not be disturbed. Choose a time for the practice that does not compromise your digestion – wait two hours after a light meal or a minimum of four hours after a full one. This is your treat, your gift to yourself, so that you can enjoy emotional and physical good health!

If you have never tried to do yoga before or are not particularly supple, don't worry. Our model was not an expert and you may not be either. Just follow the instructions carefully and do the best you can.

Salute to the sun (see pages 124–5)

trikonasana the triangle

The Triangle posture is perfect for Ones. Not only does it give an excellent stretch to the gall bladder and liver meridians, which control anger, but it also encourages flexibility of the spine, and the mind tends to follow. Additionally there is a strong compression on the colon, which aids elimination and helps us let go of resentments. Therefore, it is of benefit not only to the One, but also to any of us who are struggling with anger or resentment, and for flexibility of mind and body.

Instructions and affirmation

Repeat to yourself as you hold the posture:
I release the tension in my body and in my mind. I am open to all possibilities.

1 Stand with your legs a comfortable distance apart – enough to give them a stretch without painful straining – feet facing forward, heels in line. You are aiming toward forming an equilateral triangle: in other words, the space between your legs should ultimately be the same as the length of your legs.

2 Inhale, turning both feet toward the right, but keep your hips square to the front (in the manner of an Egyptian frieze). Exhale.

BENEFITS

❖ Provides a strong stretch to the rib cage and legs, improving flexibility and releasing blocks on the gallbladder and liver meridians.
❖ This is one of the few postures that promotes sideways flexibility of the spine.
❖ The strong compression on the abdomen helps elimination and can cure constipation.
❖ Opens the hips.
❖ Builds stamina.
❖ Promotes flexibility of mind.
❖ Trims the waist.

3 Keeping the feet and hips in the same position, inhale, raising your arms sideways to shoulder height, palms facing downward.

PRECAUTIONS

❖ Although this posture can cure sciatica (where the nerve is trapped by the spine) you should then stretch only the painful side; contracting it will make it worse.
❖ It is very important to keep the hips square to the front, or the posture will turn into a forward bend instead of a side bend and you will lose the benefit of the stretch on the gallbladder and liver meridians, and the side stretch of the spinal vertebrae.
❖ The temptation will be to take the lower arm down too far, which pulls the left hip forward and turns it into a forward bend. Just go down as far as is comfortable, keeping the hips square to the front.
❖ It is important always to go down to the right first, compressing the right side of the colon first to aid elimination.

4 Exhale, bending from the waist down to the right, letting your right arm stretch down and touch your leg. The left arm stays in line with your shoulders and reaches up to the ceiling, palm facing the front. Look up at your left hand, if you can do so without strain. Breathe quietly if you are holding the posture.

5 When you are ready to come back up, use an inhalation to help you return to the starting position; exhale, lowering the arms. Repeat three times in the same direction. Release the legs, and give them a shake. Repeat three times on the left side.

yoga mudra symbol of yoga

Yoga Mudra, with its strong stretch to the arms and shoulders, releases blocks in the meridians of the Fire Element: heart, small intestine, three heater, and pericardium, which are often implicated in type Two behavior. An additional benefit is the compression on the stomach and spleen with the forward bend, thus working on the Earth Element, which is also significant for many Twos.

Instructions and affirmation

Repeat to yourself as you hold the posture:

I nurture my own growth. I am grateful for all that others give me.

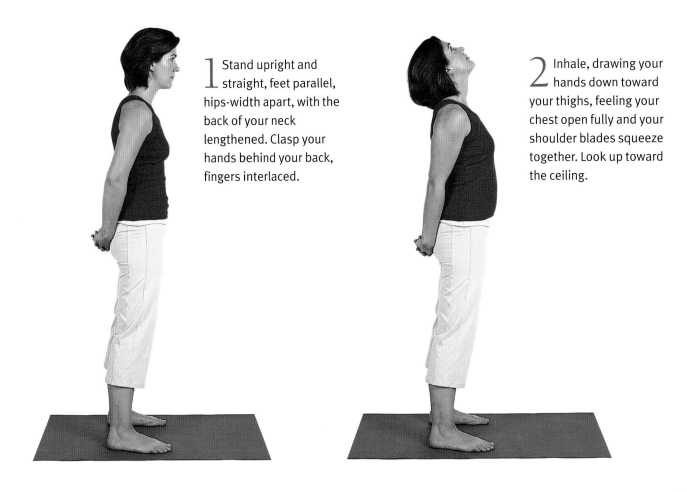

1 Stand upright and straight, feet parallel, hips-width apart, with the back of your neck lengthened. Clasp your hands behind your back, fingers interlaced.

2 Inhale, drawing your hands down toward your thighs, feeling your chest open fully and your shoulder blades squeeze together. Look up toward the ceiling.

BENEFITS

❖ Provides a strong stretch to the heart, small intestine, three heater, and pericardium meridians, releasing blocks.
❖ Improves posture and relieves back problems.
❖ Compresses and improves circulation to the stomach and spleen and other abdominal organs.
❖ Promotes better circulation to the shoulders.
❖ Increases flexibility of shoulders, arms, and spine.
❖ Stretches the chest, hamstrings, and calves.

PRECAUTIONS

❖ Don't take your head below the level of your heart in the forward bend if you have high blood pressure.
❖ Never go beyond your comfort zone when you take your head back.
❖ Do the forward bend with knees slightly bent if you have back problems.

3 Exhale, bending forward from the hips, lifting your arms up toward your head, feeling the strong stretch on both arms and shoulders. Take your head down toward your knees as far as possible, keeping it aligned with the spine, arms raised as far as is comfortable over your head without over-straining. Hold for a few counts.

4 When you are ready to inhale, return to upright with the in-breath, release your hands, and give your arms a good shake. Stand tall and still, feeling the warmth in your shoulders and arms.

tadasana the mountain

This posture, with its stillness, is appropriate for the Threes, who usually have more than enough activity in their lives. Their challenge is to stop and to pay attention, and although I can almost hear the groans as I recommend it for them, they will gain enormous benefit by regularly practicing it. It also works strongly on the arms and opens the chest, working on the Fire Element, and in particular the heart meridian, which is so often an issue for Threes.

Instructions and affirmation

Repeat to yourself as you hold the posture:

I am grounded and balanced. I welcome stillness and quiet.

1 Stand tall with your feet hips-width apart, feet parallel, knees lightly contracted, and with your tailbone tucked in so that the spine is straight. Imagine your head being lifted by a small string from a hook at the top, and slightly to the back, of your head. This tucks the chin in very slightly and lengthens the back of your neck. Shoulders are down and square to the front.

2 Inhale, taking your hands up to the prayer position in front of your chest, keeping your elbows open and wide. Gaze ahead, and exhale and inhale for a few counts, feeling the timeless quality of the mountain and the stillness. (You can, if you choose, skip to step 4 at this point.)

BENEFITS

While holding this posture, visualize a mountain; feel stillness, strength, and continuity. Be aware of your feet firmly rooted in the earth, head/arms toward heaven. In its most simple form, the arms stay straight by your sides. It can be made stronger, and works harder on the body, if you hold your arms aloft for a few breaths.

❖ Calms the mind.
❖ The Namasté posture of hands in the prayer position opens the heart and promotes compassion.
❖ The spine is aligned and your posture is improved.
❖ Restores a sense of balance to body/mind/spirit.

PRECAUTIONS

❖ Keep the back of your neck lengthened.
❖ Make sure that your spine stays straight throughout, especially when you raise your arms.
❖ Don't forget to breathe – not forced, but quietly while you hold the pose.

3 Inhale, raising your arms above your head, and hold them there, open, shoulders down, palms facing each other, for a few breaths. (You can, if you choose, keep them in the prayer position.) Maintain a steady gaze ahead, aware of your connection to the earth as well as your stretch to the heavens, strong and quiet like a mountain.

4 Lower your arms with an out-breath down to your sides. Breathe quietly for a few moments, feeling the "mountain" energy.

the harvest moon

There is such a strong connection between the moon and our emotions, and the visualization with this posture is so beautiful, that I thought it would have particular appeal to the Fours. It also gives an extremely strong stretch to the colon and lung meridians, working on the Metal Element, which I have found relates consistently to the Four.

Instructions and affirmation

Repeat to yourself as you hold the posture:
I am steady and complete like the full moon. I lack for nothing.

1 Lie on a mat on your left side in the recovery position, with the knee of your upper leg bent up and your bottom leg stretched out straight. Hold your arms out at shoulder height in front of you, palms together. Rest your head on the floor.

BENEFITS

❖ Provides a strong stretch to the colon and lung meridians, releasing blocks.
❖ Expands the lungs and improves their capacity.
❖ One of the best postures for spinal rotation.
❖ Calms the emotions and lifts the spirits.
❖ Trims the waist.
❖ Greatly improves the flexibility of the shoulders, spine, and neck.
❖ Exercises the eye muscles.

PRECAUTIONS

❖ Your neck may feel more comfortable if it is supported on a folded T-shirt or small cushion.
❖ Don't force your moving arm down to the floor. It is better to let it happen naturally in time as the shoulder becomes more flexible.
❖ Be sure that you follow the movement with your eyes to get the added benefit for them.
❖ Don't allow your "static" shoulder to lift off the floor.

2 Inhale slowly with the movement as you describe a circle in an arc over your head with the fingers of your right hand. Leave your left hand where it lies to balance you. As you make the circle over your head, follow the moving hand with your eyes, thus rotating your neck. Visualize tracing a circle around a shining full moon. (At a certain point, usually as your hand reaches above your head, you may need to lift it from the floor. That is all right; flexibility increases in time.)

3 As your hand follows on around toward your hip, you should naturally begin to exhale, and you will lose sight of your hand. Just let it flow on around, slowly gliding over your hip and back to the start position. Repeat three times, maintaining the image of a shining moon.

setu bandhasana the bridge

The Bridge, sometimes referred to as the Shoulder Bow or the Back Strengthener, is an excellent posture to work on the Water Element, balancing the expression of fear, especially when counterposed, as here, with the Gas Ejector. There is a strong compression on the kidneys while the posture is held. As the kidney meridian is largely responsible for our energy levels (see Chapter Two), this posture is extremely beneficial to the low-energy "Fear-type" Fives. Additionally, it helps Fives with an imbalance in the Metal Element (self-worth and money issues) by opening the lungs and the emotional center (see Chapter Four).

Instructions and affirmation

Repeat to yourself as you hold the posture:

I open my heart to others and welcome my emotions.

1 Lie on a nonslip mat on the floor (barefoot is safest), bend your knees, and place your feet hips-width apart, about 12 in (30 cm) from your buttocks. Extend the back of your neck, chin tucked slightly in. Arms are by your sides, palms down.

BENEFITS

❖ Works on the kidney and bladder meridians, balancing the Water Element and fear.
❖ Cleanses the kidneys and thyroid gland.
❖ Balances the hormone system.
❖ Greatly improves the flexibility and strength of the spine.
❖ Improves flexibility of the shoulders if you use your arms.
❖ Increases strength in the legs.
❖ Tones legs and buttocks.
❖ Works on the Metal Element by opening the chest.
❖ Relieves tension in the neck.
❖ Releases the emotions.

PRECAUTIONS

❖ Make sure your feet don't slip on the mat. Keeping them close to the buttocks will help ensure this does not happen.
❖ If you are holding the posture, keep breathing quietly and evenly.
❖ Warm up your back before starting the sequence by performing little tilts, rocking the pelvis.

2 Inhale, tilting your pelvis, pressing out the natural curve of your spine into the mat. Start to peel your spine off the mat, vertebra by vertebra from the tailbone, until your hips are raised right off the mat and your chin is tucked into your chest. Your breath should be timed with the movement. (You can make the posture stronger, and give more work to the Metal Element, by taking your arms up over your head and down to the floor behind you as you come up. Time them to arrive as your back is fully extended. Your arms will have to move faster than your back.) Breathe quietly while you hold the posture.

3 When you are ready to come down, inhale, and then exhale as you lower your spine (and arms if you raised them) smoothly onto the mat from the neck down to the tail, vertebra by vertebra, just as if you are wallpapering and don't want to trap any bubbles. Again, the movement should be timed with your breath.

4 Repeat the posture three times, then counterpose by inhaling, curling the spine in the opposite direction by holding your shins, and drawing your knees in toward your chest, and your forehead toward your knees as you exhale. Relax, inhaling, and repeat three times. Stretch out and relax.

virabhadrasana the warrior sequence

The Warrior Sequence builds courage. It can be used by any of us facing fearful situations, such as interviews or examinations, but it is particularly beneficial for the Six, core-fear type, to practice regularly. The legs and back receive a strong stretch, working on the bladder and kidney meridians, as does the movement of the back in the forward bend, strengthening the Water Element. But more than anything else, if the posture is practiced with the affirmations at each stage, it produces a feeling that you are strong enough to conquer the world!

Instructions and affirmation (WITH EACH POSTURE)

1 Stand with your legs apart, ideally forming an equilateral triangle, with the space between your feet the same as the length of your legs. Your hips should be square to the front, feet facing forward. Inhale, raising your arms up above your head until the palms touch, and making sure your shoulders stay down. Silently repeat the affirmation: *Arise, great Warrior; I will kill with the sword of wisdom, the fear born of ignorance.*

2 Keeping your arms extended, turn both feet and the hips to the right, exhale and repeat:
I will turn and face my fear.

BENEFITS

❖ Greatly improves courage.
❖ Works strongly on the kidney and bladder meridians and the Water Element.
❖ Builds strength in legs, ankles, and arms.
❖ Tones arms and legs.
❖ Improves balance and focus.
❖ Improves flexibility in legs, back, arms, and ankles.

PRECAUTIONS

❖ Make sure your feet have a good grip, preferably using a "sticky" yoga mat.
❖ Take your legs only as wide as your comfort zone will allow.
❖ Keep the knee at a right angle when you bend, to protect the joint.
❖ Don't take your head below heart level if you have high blood pressure.

3 Bend your right knee until it is directly over the ankle, and inhale as you take your arms down to shoulder height, facing forward over the knee. Feel strong as you look along your extended right arm, and repeat:
I will bend and let my fear pass through me.

4 Relax your back and arms down, exhaling as you fold over your bent right leg, and repeat:
I will relax and let my fear flow over me.

5 Straighten the right leg, coming back to position 2. Inhale and repeat:
And then I will arise and turn the inner eye, and where my fear has been there will be nothing.

6 Turn back to face the front, feet facing forward. Exhaling, lower your arms to shoulder level, and repeat:
Only I will remain, and I am eternity observing itself in a mirror.

| **vrikshasana** the tree

In the kinetic world of the Seven it helps for them to find steadiness, and constancy, by centering with a balance posture. I chose the Tree posture because it has the additional benefit for Sevens of giving a strong stretch to the kidney meridian, which controls fear. Vrikshasana promotes a sense of being grounded.

Instructions and affirmation

Repeat to yourself as you hold the posture:
I am steady and constant. I acknowledge my fears.

1 Stand tall and gaze at a single, steady point. Transfer your weight onto your left foot and bend up your right knee, and use your hands to place your foot as near as you can to your crotch. Don't worry if you can't get it that high – there is no competition in yoga. You can start as low as your toe just touching the floor and raise it higher over the weeks. Bring your hands into the prayer position. Breathe quietly.

BENEFITS

❖ Works on the kidney meridian and, therefore, the Water Element and fear.
❖ Lengthens the spine.
❖ Centers and improves concentration.
❖ Balances body/mind/spirit.
❖ Builds strength in the arms and legs.
❖ Improves flexibility of the hip joints, knees, and inner thighs.
❖ Strengthens the hip joint and knees, as well as the ankles.

PRECAUTIONS

❖ Stand on an even surface for stability.
❖ Bare feet are essential for this posture.
❖ Don't poke out your opposite hip to maintain balance. Keep the supporting leg lifted out of the hip and straight by imagining a line running down the center of your body.

2 When you are steady and balanced, inhale, raising your arms up over your head, hands meeting in the prayer position. Breathe steadily while you hold the posture. Your arms, if you prefer, can stay at shoulder height, or open in a V-shape overhead – whatever works best for you. Keep holding the posture for as long as is comfortable, but if you start to wobble, come out of the pose before you fall out of it. Repeat on the other side.

uttanasana standing forward bend

Eights tend to face the world with their bellies, which in time leads to a contraction in the small of the back and a slackening of the abdominal muscles. The Standing Forward Bend corrects this posture and provides a strong stretch to the legs and, therefore, the liver and gallbladder meridians. The additional movement holding the toes and opening the chest is especially good for the gallbladder and liver organs. Overall, strong work on the Wood Element helps Eights defuse anger and the rest of us express it appropriately.

Instructions and affirmation

Repeat to yourself as you hold the posture:
I relax and open to my softer self. I open my heart to receive love from others.

1 Stand tall, with your feet hips-width apart, and, inhaling, raise your arms forward and up above your head.

2 Exhale, hinging forward from the hips. Keep your head and neck in line with your spine, arms level with your ears, and as you continue the out-breath go down as far as you can without strain. If you have back problems you may want to bend your knees a little. Hold the forward bend for a few breaths, keeping your arms and neck relaxed.

3 Tuck your fingers under your toes and, tugging on them, slightly raise your head and arch your back to feel the extra stretch on the back of your legs and your chest opening. You can bend your knees if you have to. Look forward as far as is comfortable for your neck. Hold for three breaths. Relax down again.

4 Come out of the posture by breathing in, taking your arms up in front of you until they are level with your ears, and straighten up from the hips. If you have a bad back, you can come out of the posture with legs bent, uncurling the spine from the base and with arms relaxed. Breathe out, taking your arms back down to your sides. Repeat the posture three times.

BENEFITS

❖ Works on the liver and gallbladder meridians or the Wood Element to control anger.
❖ Gives a strong stretch to the bladder meridian.
❖ Makes the spine more flexible.
❖ Corrects posture, particularly a "sway" back.
❖ Strengthens the abdominal muscles and flattens the stomach.
❖ Relieves lower back pain.
❖ Improves circulation.
❖ Good for the complexion.
❖ Stretches hamstrings and calf muscles that have become contracted through wearing high heels.

PRECAUTIONS

❖ Keep your knees bent as you go down if you have a bad back.
❖ Make sure the back is level (think of balancing a tray on it) as you go up and down. It is good to have a friend check your position until you get used to what "flat" feels like.
❖ Don't take your head lower than your heart if you have high blood pressure.
❖ Be careful not to tilt your head back too far when you look forward in the extra stretch.
❖ Leave out the extra stretch if your back says no.

surya namaskar salute to the sun

For the Nines, who find getting into action difficult and who so often lack energy, there is no better sequence than the Salute to the Sun. Nothing equals it for energizing the entire body, all the meridians, and for generating a feeling of strength and balance. As a bonus, it works strongly on the legs and torso, releasing blocks on the gall bladder and liver meridians and, therefore, the Wood Element, helping Nines express anger and find direction. It is thus a particularly appropriate sequence for Nines to practice first thing in the morning, and for any of us who are sluggish at this time of day. It can also be used as a warm-up sequence before doing any of the other postures.

Instructions and affirmation

Repeat to yourself as you do the sequence:

I am energized and ready for action. I greet the day with enthusiasm.

1 Stand with your feet and legs together, hands in the prayer position, elbows out. Inhale and exhale once.

2 Inhale, raising your arms over your head, arching your back as far as is comfortable. Keep your arms level with your ears, knees locked, and feet on the mat.

3 Exhaling, hinge forward from the hips, placing your hands on either side of your feet, touching the floor.

4 Inhaling, stretch your right leg behind you as far as you can, right knee on the floor and toes of the right foot curled under. Look up and arch your back, looking forward in a "starting-block" position.

5 Exhale, taking your left foot back to join the right, straightening the right knee. Both feet and legs are now together and straight, arms also straight, hands flat on the mat, forming the "plank" posture.

6 Exhaling, lower your knees to the mat. Take your buttocks toward your heels and your chest down to the mat to sweep it forward through your arms. Inhale

up into the Raised Cobra position. Your arms should be straight, hips and thighs on the mat, head looking straight forward.

7 Tuck your toes under, exhale, and push your hips up into the Dog pose. Push your hips back, taking your head between your arms, helping your feet to go flat.

8 Inhale, taking your right foot forward between your hands, back into the "starting-block" position, but with the other knee bent.

9 Bring your left foot forward to join the right, exhale, straightening your legs (if possible) into the forward bend. Place your hands alongside your feet (if possible).

10 Inhale, coming up with a straight back. Arch back once more with your arms above your head.

11 Return to the start position, exhaling, palms together in the prayer position in front of your chest. Reverse the sequence on the other side, then repeat on both sides, alternating at least three times.

1   2   3   4   5

6   7

8   9   10   11

BENEFITS

- ❖ Balances and activates all the meridians.
- ❖ Increases energy.
- ❖ Improves circulation and brings vitality to the entire body.
- ❖ Strengthens lung function.
- ❖ Improves muscle tone throughout the body.
- ❖ Tones the digestive system.
- ❖ Flexes the spine.
- ❖ Balances the hormones working on the endocrine glands.
- ❖ Helps to regulate the menstrual cycle.
- ❖ Relieves stress and tension.
- ❖ Benefits and tones the skin.
- ❖ Corrects posture.

PRECAUTIONS

- ❖ If you have uncontrolled high blood pressure, do not take your head below the heart in postures. Consult a properly qualified yoga teacher for alternatives.
- ❖ As with all yoga, never perform it on a full stomach. Allow 2 hours after a light meal; 4 hours after a full meal.
- ❖ It is better to avoid doing this sequence just before bedtime.
- ❖ It's better to have the leg vertical, and to protect the knee by keeping it directly above the ankle.

CROWN CHAKRA
on and slightly above the crown

BROW CHAKRA
middle of the brow

THROAT CHAKRA
throat

HEART CHAKRA
between the breasts

SOLAR PLEXUS CHAKRA
two finger widths above and below the navel

SACRAL CHAKRA
genitals

ROOT CHAKRA
at base of spine

CHAPTER FOUR

The chakras

The Glory of the divine,
The Spirit's guiding light,
The infinite wisdom of the universe:
All are embedded in the body.

Your body is the earthly garment
Of the heavenly spirit.

Yogi Amrit Desai

introduction to the chakras

We have taken an Enneagram journey through the mind and the body to arrive at the chakra system, where the innermost potential for personal development and spirituality is forged. *Chakra* is the Sanskrit word for "wheel"; in this case, it refers to seven main vortices of energy, vibrating and spinning like wheels, aligned with the spine centrally up the body. The first is at the tip of the coccyx, and the others rise in stages to the crown of the head. When we sit or stand correctly, spine aligned, it enables a free flow of energy between chakras up a central column, known as the Sushumna, and two separate and intertwining streams of Sakti/Siva or yin/yang energy known as Ida and Pingala, which coil around them like snakes. These seven chakras are messengers between different levels of consciousness, layered over us like shades placed on a lamp.

Whereas the acupuncture points are minor centers where Chi energy may be stimulated with needles, massage, or postures, the seven main chakras are where prime concentrations of Chi/Prana emanate from the central core of our bodies and project outward. They are like a series of doorways with keys to our development through life. These spheres of radiant energy are clearly visible to clairvoyants, but all of us can experience Prana. Rub your hands together vigorously and then hold them in front of you about 2 feet (80 cm) apart, palms facing each other. Close your eyes and move your palms slowly toward each other until you feel resistance. If you focus, you will feel something like an invisible balloon between your hands. Play with it – this is your radiant energy! It completely surrounds and protects you. Keep testing the resistance. You have just experienced in a small way the energy that is concentrated in the chakras.

Knowledge of the chakras used to be withheld from lay people in the West, perhaps because the subtleties of the system are not easy to transmit in words: true understanding can be gained only experientially. It is highly intricate and complex; any attempt to put into words the power of the chakras can be only partially successful. Nevertheless, a basic understanding of their

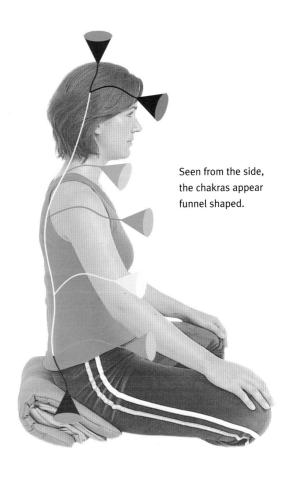

Seen from the side, the chakras appear funnel shaped.

energies undoubtedly helps to deepen psychospiritual knowledge, and should not, I feel, be denied students of the Enneagram. However, never underestimate their power and always treat this knowledge with great respect.

If you have never tried to do yoga before or are not particularly supple, don't worry. Our model was not an expert and you may not be either. Just follow the instructions carefully and do the best you can.

As you can see from the illustration opposite, the Root Chakra opens downward, sending energy from the tip of the spine toward the center of the earth. The following five project energy forward, the Crown Chakra upward toward the heavens. It is the energy of the chakras, represented as a coiled serpent at the base of the spine, that is consciously raised in the practice of kundalini, or tantric yoga. (This is an advanced yoga practice to achieve enlightenment.) Although it is more likely for chakras to open, and blocks to be freed, without conscious effort, I will guide you through each chakra in turn and relate them to your Enneagram type, so that you can identify possible weaknesses and learn ways to strengthen them.

I believe we develop in life through the chakras, starting with the lowest vibrational energy of the Root Chakra between 0 and 7 years of age, when security is our main concern. There follows a flowering of creativity and sexual energy (much earlier than most parents wish to admit) from between about 7 and 14 years, triggered by the energy of the second chakra, in the area of the genitals. Next, we develop our personal power in the outside world (finding jobs, forging a career, and so on), when the focus is in the Solar Plexus Chakra.

It is said that from here on the opening of the chakras can occur only through grace, not by conscious effort. When the energy rises to the Heart Chakra, we move into a time for parenting, or giving out to the world, which I believe lasts for many years, until our 50s, when energy tends to concentrate in the Throat Chakra, which rules communication. This is when many of us feel the spontaneous urge to express ourselves at a deeper, more meaningful level (something I have seen again and again among my patients and friends, men and women, as they

reach menopause). Intuitions increase when energy concentrates in the Brow Chakra, and there is awareness of true essence, of connection with the universal, divine energy of the cosmos experienced in the Crown Chakra.

Life, inevitably, imposes blips in this natural progression, creating blocks. Imagine an infant who is neglected and experiences insecurity, or a child whose creativity is stifled, or their delicate unfolding sexual awareness poisoned by guilt; the energy in the first two chakras may not have the chance to flower. (The symbols of the chakras all have petals.) There may be a gross distortion of power if the young adult cannot get work or establish him/herself in the world. (I believe this may in part explain the compulsion for rival fans to fight at football matches, or for young people to join gangs or extremist groups.) Parenting may not come naturally; there may be more take from the world than give. What if communication is stifled, or insights derided, or the connection with spirituality mocked? All the chakras have value, the lower as much as the higher. A block in any chakra will, to an extent, affect all the others.

Each of the chakras is relevant to all of the Enneagram types; however, at the end of each description I identify specific ways I believe the chakras may be affected by type behavior.

Caution
You should close each session meditating/doing postures to open the chakras with something that grounds you and protects you before you go out into the outside world. Touch the floor or feel your back grounded on the floor. Then imagine a clear bubble of light that surrounds and protects you and seal it so the bubble lets only the good vibes in.

muladhara the root chakra

mula = root *adhara* = support

Location
At the tip of the coccyx, opening downward toward the center of the earth. Some say at the cervix for women, the perineum for men.

Purpose
This chakra is connected with our most primitive desire for security, survival, and connection with our tribe/family. This is our foundation. The newborn infant and small child require that their basic needs for shelter, food, and drink be met. Beyond that, the child needs to be held, to be enfolded in love. Studies of chimps deprived of this show them failing to thrive and becoming depressed.

The energy of Muladhara governs our ambition, self-expression, primitive responses to life's threats, fears, and consistency. It is associated with the physical body, vibrates at the lowest level, and yet is the seat of the dormant kundalini energy, gateway to the Siva/Sakti polarity, and needs to connect with the Crown Chakra, Sahasrara, through the other chakras.

Color
This chakra glows a clear, bright red, like the fiery core of the earth.

Element
Earth: the earth nourishes us and provides all that we need for our growth.

Sense
This chakra governs our ability to smell. It is activated by smell, as when we light incense or a scented candle.

Symbol
The symbol for this chakra has four petals, an elephant for strength and endurance, and representations of Sakti and Siva. Muladhara is also associated with the bull and the ox. This chakra reminds us of our animal, instinctive nature.

Age
From birth until around 7 or 8 years of age.

Physical connections
Muladhara rules the legs, feet, and all solid body parts: spine, bones, teeth, nails. It also rules the anus, rectum, colon and the prostate, blood, and the building of cells.

Glands
Adrenals: the fight or flight response is elicited in the Root Chakra. Animals often defecate or urinate when they are very afraid and flee, or, filled with adrenalin, they fight. This chakra also governs the kidney function.

Astrological connections
Aries, **Mars** Primordial life energy, the power to achieve, aggressiveness, birth.
Taurus Connection to the earth, stability, sense pleasure, possessions.
Capricorn, **Saturn** Structure, stability.

Sound
Tribal music, drumming, monotonous emphatic rhythms, sounds of nature.

Vowel
"O," as in "rope."

Mantra
LAM

Gemstones
Agate, hematite, bloodstone, garnet, red coral, ruby, smoky quartz, tiger eye.

Aromatherapy oils
Cypress, marjoram, myrrh.

Balanced energy in Muladhara
We will feel secure, loved, supported by the earth, comfortable in our families. There will be a deep connection with the earth and an appreciation for nature and an attunement with its cycles. It is easy to achieve goals, and there will be a primordial trust – a belief in the world as a secure and supportive place. There is a sense of gratitude for earth's gifts and optimism about its bounty.

Unbalanced or blocked energy in Muladhara
Physically there may be constipation, diarrhea, hemorrhoids, tremor, foot problems, and so on.

Emotionally, the world is a fearful place, and the perception is that people are out to harm us. We mistrust support from the earth. Attention revolves around money and possessions and the fear of losing them. It may be difficult to be generous or to receive. People become inconsistent, jumpy, and undependable. There can be an obsession with dirt and germs. Emotions may swing between being very sweet, to vicious cruelty, to the point of self-harm or injury to others, and there may be excessive risk-taking behavior.

Suggested imbalance in Muladhara through the nine Enneagram types

One When there is obsession with cleanliness. Anal-retentive nature, constipation.

Two If the Two is excessively needy, and clingy in relationships.

Three When acquisitiveness becomes all-consuming, or when ambition drives them to disregard others.

Four When the Four swings wildly between emotions, or rejects their "tribe."

Five Avarice/stinginess is an indication of imbalance in this chakra.

Six When fear rules, this chakra is often unbalanced in Sixes.

Seven When there is a complete lack of grounding, of earth.

Eight When aggression is out of control.

Nine When a Nine spaces out, and becomes ungrounded or lacks structure, or when anxious in their stress point (Six).

Suggestions for balancing Muladhara

- Get your hands in the soil, even if it is just growing a potted plant.
- Wear red, especially red underwear.
- Hold one of the associated gemstones, or put them on your body near the Root Chakra.
- Repeat the mantra LAM.
- Play tribal music. Take up drumming.
- Walk barefoot on the grass.
- Sing "O" in lower C.
- Sit and watch the sunrise or sunset, aware of your tailbone touching the ground.
- Hug a tree.
- Before each meal, silently give thanks to Mother Nature for supporting you.
- Scent your room/clothes with the associated oils.
- Stay in – hole up indoors.
- Cook yourself nutritious, wholesome food, especially root vegetables.
- Fix your roof or anything else about your home that might generate feelings of insecurity.
- When you feel the spontaneous instinct to give, follow it.
- Spend time out of doors in nature.

Posture and meditation to activate Muladhara

Seated postures activate this chakra, particularly on the ground.

EASY SITTING POSE

1 Sit on the ground with a firm cushion under your buttocks, back straight, and bend your left knee and tuck the left heel into your groin.

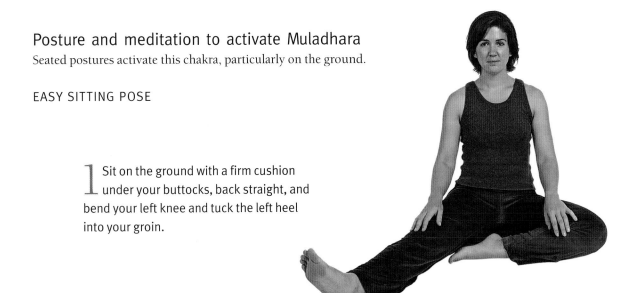

BENEFITS

❖ Improves flexibility of the inner thighs and the hips.
❖ Activates Muladhara.
❖ Brings a feeling of security and trust.

2 Bend your right knee and place your right foot in front of your left, crossing your legs.

3 Slip slightly forward on the meditation cushion, or "zafu," until your knees open comfortably to the floor. Support them with more cushions if necessary. Don't sit square on the cushion with knees raised (above right).

4 Place your right hand in your left, thumbs touching, and let your shoulders relax. Keep the spine straight.

5 Close your eyes, breathe quietly for a few minutes and repeat the affirmation:
I am grateful for the earth's support. I am secure and unafraid.

Svadisthana the sacral chakra

sva = that which is itself
dhisthana = one's own abode/
home of the self or sweetness

Location
In the lower abdomen between the navel and the genitals.

Purpose
The second meaning of dhisthana above gives the best clue to the energy of this chakra – for here lies our ability to experience sweetness in our lives. Not just on an animal level, in the sex act, but through creativity generally. This chakra connects strongly with the fifth, which also rules creativity, but on a higher level. Here the creativity is more primordial, more personal. Svadisthana is also very close to the first chakra, and some functions are the same.

Svadisthana helps us to flower in sexuality and in the joyous union with our creativity.

Color
This chakra is a vibrant orange, which encourages self-esteem.

Element
Water: the free flowing of emotions like water, and the flushing out of impurities.

Sense
As you might imagine: taste. Our ability to taste the sweetness of life, guilt free and with enthusiasm.

Symbol
A six-petaled lotus. Within, a shining crescent moon and an image of a makara – a coiled, fish-tailed alligator.

Age
Peaks from around 8 to 14 years of age.

Physical connections
Svadisthana rules the pelvis, reproductive organs, womb, kidneys, bladder. It also rules fluids, such as blood, sperm, lymph, and gastric juices.

Glands
The ovaries, prostate, and testicles.

Astrological connections
Pluto Creative transformation.
Moon/Cancer Receptivity, emotionality, and fertility.
Libra/Venus Sensuality, creativity, and aesthetics.
Scorpio Desire.

Sound
Flowing music, belly dance music, couples dancing, folk music, and salsa. In nature: birdsong, flowing water, and fountains.

Vowel
"O," as in "November," sung in the key of D.

Mantra
VAM

Gemstones
Carnelian, moonstone, citrine, golden topaz, tourmaline.

Aromatherapy oils
Ylang-ylang, sandalwood, jasmine, rose, and petigrain.

Balanced energy in Svadisthana
The archetype is of a sovereign child, full of innocent wonder and delight in the world, with an enthusiasm for life and awe at its beauty. Sexuality is expressed naturally

and without guilt. Relationships with the opposite sex are comfortable and appropriately expressed. They are considerate, open, kind, and friendly and feel a deep joy in life. They are creative.

Unbalanced or blocked energy in Svadisthana

Sexual expression is inhibited or inappropriate and misdirected. There may be excessive fantasies, coarse sexuality, coldness, or emotional paralysis. There may be an inability to take life's knocks and see them creatively as part of the whole. The archetype is of the isolated martyr – full of mistrust in the world, of uncertainty, with a pessimistic outlook.

Physically, there may be sexual difficulties, such as impotence/frigidity, as well as kidney or bladder problems, low back pain, fibroids, ovarian cysts, and prostate problems.

Suggested imbalance in Svadisthana through the nine Enneagram types

One   When judgment turns against sexuality – the prim zealot.

Two   When martyrdom takes over; sexual aggression in the search for love.

Three   Overworking and denying enjoyment of life, low sex drive.

Four   When they are on a high, over-the-top awe, or when creativity is stifled by overwhelming depression.

Five   If there is repressed sexuality and where there is emotional withholding.

Six   Fear inhibiting the flowering of a sexual/intimate relationship.

Seven   Denial of fear can endanger Sevens when seeking intimate relationship; avoiding intimacy to keep their options open.

Eight   Lust is a distortion of this energy when extreme.

Nine   Denying their own creativity and sexual expression to go along with that of their lover, resulting in frustration.

Suggestions for balancing Svadisthana

- Make time in your life for creativity in a way that you enjoy.
- Spend time with the opposite sex.
- Acknowledge the treasures of the earth.
- Spend time in nature, particularly by water – near fountains, rivers, the sea, or waterfalls.
- Explore creativity in your sex life with your partner.
- If you are a woman, think about how you could express your male side creatively.
- If you are a man, think about how you could express your female side creatively.
- Wear orange, particularly orange underwear.
- Sing "O" in the key of D.
- Repeat the mantra VAM.
- Lie down with one of the associated gemstones on your lower abdomen.
- Listen to the appropriate music; join a class for couples dancing. Women, take up belly dancing.
- Scent your bath with a selection of the associated oils.
- Spend time with friends who freely express delight in the world.

Visualization

1 Sit in a comfortable position, ensuring that your spine is straight. If you sit in a chair do not cross your legs, and make sure your feet are supported by the floor. If you are sitting cross-legged, you may find that your knees relax better toward the floor with a firm cushion or a foam block under your buttocks. A meditation cushion, or "zafu," is best, because you can slide to the front of it, which helps the knees go down and also helps keep the spine in the correct position (see the pictures on page 133). Focus on the breath for a few minutes.

2 Now breathe as if right down to the lower abdomen and visualize a clear, bright orange light glowing forward from the spine at a level with the sacrum.

3 Fill your abdomen with the orange light, and allow any pleasurable sensations to happen.

4 Stay with the light, breathing quietly, imagining it getting stronger with each out-breath.

5 Repeat to yourself three times: *I welcome and accept all my emotions. My life is full of creative opportunities.*

6 Return to normal, quiet breathing and come out of the meditation by listening to the sounds around you. Open your eyes when you are ready.

Yoga posture to stimulate Svadisthana

THE LOCUST – SHALABASANA

1 Lie facedown, legs together, chin on the mat, arms by your side, hands tucked under your thighs with the palms up.

2 Inhale, point your toes, and raise your legs. Use your fingers to help, lifting your legs as high as you can without bending them or taking your hips off the mat. Maintain the pose for a few moments, if possible, breathing quietly; exhale as you return to the start position. Repeat three times.

3 Counterpose by resting for a while, breathing quietly, in the Child Pose.

BENEFITS

❖ Activates Svadisthana.
❖ Improves circulation.
❖ Greatly strengthens the lower back.
❖ Tones the buttocks and the backs of the thighs.
❖ Energizes the nervous system.

PRECAUTIONS

❖ Do this one leg at a time if your back prefers, until you get stronger.
❖ You can have your legs slightly apart if that is more comfortable for you.

Manipura the solar plexus chakra

manipura = city of jewels

Location
Emanating forward from a level of the spine between the 12th thoracic and the 1st lumbar vertebrae. Expanding approximately to two finger widths above and below the navel.

Purpose
Manipura controls our personal power, our will, helping us find a point of balance between tyrannical assertiveness and passive submission, and establish our social identity.

   The archetype is the spiritual warrior, setting forth with courage into the wider world to seek his fortune, as opposed to the drudge, daunted by such a journey.

Color
Yellow: encourages confidence.

Element
Fire: attractive, warming, purifying.

Sense
Sight: note the connection with the liver, which rules sight in the five-element system.

Symbol
A ten-petaled lotus, a Ram, known for its fiery nature.

Age
From between about 14 and 21 years of age, traditionally the time when young people go out into the working world and, as all parents know, have a great need to assert themselves as individuals.

Physical connections
Digestive system, liver, gall bladder, spleen, stomach, abdomen, lower back, autonomic nervous system.

Glands
This chakra rules the pancreas.

Astrological connections
Leo/Sun Need to be recognized, be powerful, to have status. Warmth and strength.
Sagittarius/Jupiter Expansion, taking ideas out into the world. Wisdom.
Virgo/Mercury Selfless service in the world, ability to analyze, conform. Communication.
Mars Energy, willingness to move into action, self-assertiveness.

Sound
Bold, orchestral music, or relaxing music. Tibetan overtone chanting.

Vowel
"O," as in "god," sung in the key of E.

Mantra
RAM

Gemstones
Amber, tiger eye, yellow citrine and topaz, agate, aventurine, sunstone.

Aromatherapy oils
Bergamot, ylang-ylang, cinnamon, chamomile, lemon, thyme, vetiver.

Balanced energy in Manipura
We are strong, confident, and sure of our position in the world, welcome challenges and deal with them well. There is equal respect for oneself and others. If there is a strong connection between this chakra, the Brow Chakra, and the Crown Chakra your desires may be

achieved. Named the City of Jewels, it is said that strength in Manipura enables you to locate hidden treasure. I would interpret this to mean deeper spiritual treasure.

There is a calm strength recognizable in people who are balanced in this chakra, and equilibrium between spiritual and material.

Unbalanced or blocked energy in Manipura

Physically there may be digestive problems, diabetes, ulcers, eating disorders such as bulimia or anorexia, or excessive eating and a bloated stomach. There may also be sight problems. Emotionally, the person may be overly dominant, aggressive, and pushy, or meek, unassertive, and unable to stick up for themselves. Often discouraged, they see life as full of obstacles; they lack fire and enthusiasm.

Excess energy here can lead to an undue emphasis on material things, and workaholic, angry, or controlling behavior. Too little, and there may be fear of being alone, insecurity, and the need for constant reassurance.

It is said that a block at this chakra prevents an opening of the higher chakras.

Suggested imbalance in Manipura through the nine Enneagram types

One   When controlling behavior takes over.

Two   The habit of deferring to a dominant other, giving away personal power.

Three   The Three at their most materialistic, dominant, and least empathetic.

Four   When they are disempowered by their sense of worthlessness and give up the fight.

Five   When they become too superior and when they hide from the world.

Six   The lack of courage, fearing to assert themselves in the world.

Seven   When they deny fear and act recklessly through false courage or overconfidence.

Eight   When they are over-dominant and aggressive. Often unbalanced in Eights.

Nine   The lack of energy, inability to get into action, and passive aggression.

Suggestions for balancing Manipura

- Build a bonfire and sit around it with friends.
- Wear yellow – a gold-colored belt or a scarf.
- Put a drop of one of the aromatherapy oils in your navel. (Do not go out in the sun with bergamot on your skin.)
- Sunbathe (taking obvious precautions).
- Take a class in Tibetan overtone chanting.
- Chant the mantra RAM.
- Sing "O" in the key of E.
- Regularly ask yourself, "How do I use power?"
- Think of a powerful/humble person whom you admire, and mirror their qualities.
- Watch the sunrise and the sunset.
- Do the Salute to the Sun (see pages 124–25) each morning before breakfast.
- Lie down and relax with one of the associated gemstones on your navel.

Visualization

1 Sit in your comfortable meditation posture, close your eyes, and breathe quietly for a few minutes, focusing on the rise and fall of the belly as you do so.

2 Now imagine you are walking, on a glorious sunny day, into the middle of a huge field of sunflowers.

3 Look around you at the golden field, drinking in the sight of all the yellow sunflowers, and enjoy the warmth on your body.

4 Your attention is caught by one particular sunflower. Gently holding its bloom in your hand, gaze into its center, feeling its strength and brilliance radiate out toward you.

5 As you gaze into the flower you feel a gradual change as you seem to become that flower, shining with its unique radiance. Enjoy the sensation for a few minutes.

6 Repeat the affirmation three times: *I am loving and appropriately powerful.*

7 Return to focusing on your breath and come out of the meditation by listening to the sounds around you. Open your eyes when you are ready.

Yoga posture to balance Manipura

TIBETAN NUMBER FOUR – ARDHA PURVOTTANASANA

This posture is one of five powerful Tibetan exercises to stimulate the chakras. Repeat this affirmation as you do it: *I enjoy quiet strength. I am full of courage.*

BENEFITS

❖ Strengthens arms, hands and wrists, back, and legs.
❖ Opens abdominal area and improves the circulation.
❖ Works on the Manipura Chakra.

PRECAUTIONS

❖ The position of your hands is very important. They must be exactly alongside the hips.
❖ If keeping your head back strains your neck, keep it tucked into the chest.

1 Sit upright on the mat with your hands flat on the mat beside your hips (hands facing forward or back, whichever is most comfortable for you). Your legs are together, chin tucked slightly in.

2 Inhale, bend your knees, and push your hips up, keeping the soles of your feet flat on the mat. Look forward, along your body, or upward, but keep your neck comfortable. (Your body forms a kind of flat tabletop.)

3 Exhale, coming back to the start position. Repeat this at least three times, increasing to five, seven, and nine repetitions as you become stronger.

anahata the heart chakra

anahata = the unstruck sound

Location
In the center of the chest, projecting forward between the breasts, from a level between the 4th and 5th vertebrae.

Purpose
The ability to express compassion and love is activated by this chakra. We talk of "heartfelt" feeling, our "hearts going out" to someone, "heartache," or a "broken heart." There is a distinct physical feeling in the heart area when we have these strong emotions, making the activity of this chakra easy to identify. Here there is a real expansion in the human spirit, the diaphragm seen in many cultures – including Mexican, Egyptian, and Middle Eastern – to be a kind of boundary between the earthly and heavenly. Think of the diaphragm like the surface of the earth with Anahata, the sun, rising above it, radiating warmth. Here the right and left polarities of the body, represented by right and left arms, meet the rising male/female energies up the chakras, forming the center of a cross.

Art, music, poetry, and the beauty of nature are transformed into feelings through the energy of Anahata. It is the seat of the devotional form of yoga, known as bhakti, which recognizes divine love.

Color
This chakra is green, also pink and gold.

Element
Air: the lungs are in the region of Anahata.

Sense
The sense associated with Anahata is touch.

Symbol
The symbol for this chakra is an upward-pointing triangle superimposed on a downward-pointing triangle contained within a 12-petaled lotus. The two triangles represent the meeting point of more instinctual animal energy with the transpersonal energies of the upper chakras. The animal is a deer/antelope.

Age
It is strongest from age 21, when focus is on providing for family in a selfless way and giving out love and emotional support, until our late 40s.

Physical connections
Heart, upper back, thorax, lungs, blood and circulation, skin, the immune system, arms, and hands.

Glands
The Heart Chakra rules the thymus.

Astrological connections
Leo/Sun Emotional warmth, generosity, and sincerity. **Libra/Venus** Contact, desire for harmony, deep appreciation of beauty. Venus rules this chakra. **Saturn** Rising above ego with selfless love.

Sound
Any music that lifts the heart – classical, chanting, hymns, devotional music, and similar types.

Vowel
"Ah," sung in the key of F.

Mantra
YAM

Gemstones
Rose quartz, watermelon tourmaline, kunzite, emerald, jade, green aventurine, malachite.

Aromatherapy oils

Attar of roses, bergamot, melissa, geranium, clary sage.

Balanced energy in Anahata

This is the person who radiates love and compassion, kindness, generosity, and tolerance, and I can give no better example than His Holiness the Dalai Lama. People with strong energy in Anahata have the natural ability to heal others; sometimes merely to be in their presence is healing. They have the ability to change the world around them, and their lives are an expression of divine love and bliss.

Unbalanced or blocked energy in Anahata

Physically, you see heart and circulation problems, lung disease such as asthma, and breathing problems. The chest may be overly armored with muscles, or somewhat collapsed looking. Emotionally, there can be a range of problems, from coldness or heartlessness with a lack of response to others, to ruthless egotistical behavior. They may feel unworthy, be dependent on others, melancholic, want to give love but fear rejection. They may give excessively, but have difficulty receiving. You can see over-friendly, gushing behavior that is indiscriminate, or problems with commitment. Love may be tainted with fierce possessiveness. Loneliness is often an issue; life may be experienced as being full of pain and sorrow.

Suggested imbalance in Anahata through the nine Enneagram types

One   When they lack compassion, particularly toward themselves.

Two   Lacking balance between giving and receiving. Much Two behavior points to an imbalance in this chakra.

Three   When feelings are denied.

Four   The emotional swings between depression and unhealthy attachment.

Five   Where there is detachment from emotions.

Six   When fear blocks compassion and makes them selfish.

Seven   At times when the focus on plans and ideas leaves no room for compassion.

Eight   The aggressive need for power over others takes over and they lack compassion and deny their soft center.

Nine   Serving others to the point of self-neglect.

Suggestions for balancing Anahata

- Practice kindness. (The Dalai Lama says his religion is "practicing kindness.")
- Learn to tune in to your heart's messages and trust them.
- One's first response is usually generous – follow it.
- Enjoy nature. Walk slowly enough to appreciate the beauty around you.
- Fill your room with pink flowers.
- Notice when you become judgmental and lack compassion.
- Place a few drops of the appropriate oil between your breasts.
- Read the poems of Rumi.
- Listen to uplifting music.
- Give a gift, and forget about doing so.
- Notice how much you receive from others.
- Write down five things that you are grateful for at the end of each day.
- Chant "ah" in the key of E, or the mantra YAM.
- Lie down and relax with one of the associated gemstones between your breasts.

Meditation/visualization

1 Kneel on the floor, back straight, eyes closed, hands resting on your thighs. (You can put a cushion under your buttocks if you like.) Relax your shoulders and concentrate on your breath. Stay like this for several minutes, until you are completely relaxed and focused.

2 Next, picture someone you love who needs healing kneeling opposite you, and imagine a line of golden light stretching along the floor between you both.

3 Now picture this light passing up your backs to join in infinity, establishing a triangle.

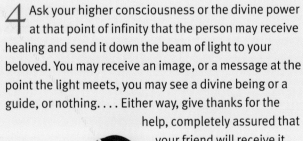

4 Ask your higher consciousness or the divine power at that point of infinity that the person may receive healing and send it down the beam of light to your beloved. You may receive an image, or a message at the point the light meets, you may see a divine being or a guide, or nothing. . . . Either way, give thanks for the help, completely assured that your friend will receive it. When you are ready, return to a focus on your breath, and come out of the meditation by listening to the sounds around you. Open your eyes when you are ready.

BENEFITS

❖ Tones and stretches the chest and upper back.
❖ Improves posture.
❖ Opens the Heart Chakra.

Yoga posture to balance Anahata

ANGEL WINGS

1 Stand erect with your feet hips-width apart. Inhale, stretching out your arms at shoulder level.

2 Exhale. Then, with your next breath, stretch your arms backward, without bending the elbows, trying to make your shoulder blades meet. Lift up your chin and raise your chest upward, feeling it expand.

3 Exhale, bringing your arms around to the front, hands touching, curving the spine slightly forward and contracting the chest muscles. Repeat several times: arms back with the inhalation, forward as you exhale, finishing with an out-breath lowering the arms.

vishuddha the throat chakra

vishuddha = to purify

Location

On a level between the 3rd cervical vertebra and the Adam's apple down to the base of the neck.

Purpose

This chakra rules communication, our ability to express our inner spirit or essence clearly and confidently. Vishuddha enables us to access divine inspiration, to be guided by and have an unshakeable trust in the true inner voice and to have a deeper understanding of life. At this level we have the potential to connect with information from subtler spheres and higher dimensions. We become conscious of our mission in life and have the ability to separate functions of lower energies from higher, giving us powers of discrimination. Connected strongly with the Sacral Chakra, Svadisthana, Vishuddha also rules creativity, but on a more spiritual level.

Color

Pale, silvery turquoise blue, like moonlight rippling on water.

Element

Ether: the element of this chakra is ether, meaning "akasha," or "astral light."

Sense

The sense associated with this chakra is hearing.

Symbol

A 16-petaled lotus encircling a downward-pointing triangle. The animal is a moon-white elephant, but this one is unrestrained by a collar.

Age

Strong in middle age, from the late 40s, when many of us feel the compulsion to express our deeper selves creatively.

Physical connections

Neck, thyroid, jaw, ears, vocal chords and voice, trachea, bronchial tubes, upper lungs, esophagus, arms, nape of the neck, nose, and teeth.

Gland

The thyroid gland.

Astrological connections

Gemini/Mercury Exchange of ideas, of knowledge, and of experience. Ruled by Mercury.
Mars Activation of self-expression.
Taurus/Venus Sensitivity to form and space.
Aquarius/Uranus Independence and divine inspiration.

Sound

Taissé chanting, Gregorian chants, mantra chanting.

Vowel

"Eh," sung in the key of G.

Mantra

HAM

Gemstones

Aquamarine, turquoise, chalcedony, celestite, sodalite, pale sapphire.

Aromatherapy oils

Sage, eucalyptus, lavender, sandalwood, neroli, chamomile, myrrh.

Balanced energy in Vishuddha

We are able to express ourselves clearly from an inner truth and, importantly, to reveal our weaknesses as well as our strengths with great honesty. We are silent when appropriate, able to speak with clarity when that is called for. Speech or written communication will be imaginative and inspiring. It will be free of judgment and prejudice, independent, and not swayed by others. (The ability to say no is strengthened by Vishuddha.) When energy is strong here there is deep joy and a sense of integrity. Telepathy is a regular occurrence.

Unbalanced or blocked energy in Vishuddha

Problems will arise from the lack of communication between mind and body. There may be thoughtless acts, difficulty in expressing true feelings, or a complete shutting off and denial of them. Speech may be blunt or coarse, businesslike without emotion, loud or too quiet to hear. There may be a torrent of words in an attempt to cover up true feelings, or the person may remain silent, fearing judgment. Creativity may be blocked.

Physically, one sees throat problems – sore throats, swollen glands, and a thyroid imbalance. There may also be neck ache, hearing problems such as tinnitus, or breathing problems such as bronchitis/asthma. Colds are often a manifestation of disturbed energy in this chakra.

Suggested imbalance in Vishuddha through the nine Enneagram types

One   When they express harsh judgments of other people, overly critical.

Two   The Two habit of changing direction midsentence when they sense that what they say is not going down too well. Failure to express their own needs.

Three   Business talk, void of feeling. Failure to listen to the inner voice when it says slow down.

Four   When they feel unworthy, that their creativity or ideas have no value.

Five   The inability to verbalize feelings as they arise.

Six   Outbursts against other people – attack as a means of defense.

Seven   The torrent of words that keeps others from sharing the exchange.

Eight   Going deaf on other people's ideas, forcing their own through.

Nine   When they are unable to verbalize their own needs, or they lack creative initiative.

Suggestions for balancing Vishuddha

- Listen on a regular basis for the inner voice. Paying attention to it makes it louder.
- Take time for reflection when the voice may be heard.
- Lie on the grass and look up at a clear blue sky and contemplate the ether.
- Wear turquoise blue – especially around the throat – as a scarf, necklace, or collar.
- Gaze at moonlight reflected on water.
- Eat fruit and pure, cleansing foods.
- After a dinner party, reflect on what you have said and how you said it.
- Become aware of the tone of voice you use, whether you need to pitch it differently.
- Notice any restrictions around the throat area. Lengthen the back of your neck, tucking in your chin from time to time throughout the day.
- Take up a hobby where your most spiritual creativity can flower.
- Look at how you might increase creativity in your work.
- Speak up for yourself.
- Next time you have a sore throat ask yourself, "What am I avoiding saying to someone?"
- Practice speaking from the heart and notice how well it is received.

Meditation

1 Choose a comfortable sitting position with a straight back, and lengthen the back of the neck. Place your hands one in another in your lap, thumbs touching. Relax your shoulders.

2 Pay attention to your breath, not altering or forcing it in any way.

3 Be aware of the cool air in your nostrils as you breathe in, the warm air on your upper lip as you breathe out. Stay with this for a few minutes.

4 Now take your attention to the breath as it passes down your windpipe and note the slight sound that it makes as it does so. Stay with this for several minutes.

5 When you are completely relaxed, drop your attention on the breath and simply listen intently to each sound as it comes to you, without expectation. After a few minutes you may become aware of a constant background sound – like white noise. This is what the yogis call *nadam*, and it is the sound of your own cells vibrating. Focus on this. When your mind wanders, gently bring it home, back to nadam. Keep this going for as long as you can.

6 When you are ready to come out of the meditation, picture a turquoise-blue light at your throat and repeat the affirmation: *I trust my inner voice and speak the truth clearly.*
Open your eyes when you are ready.

Yoga posture to activate Vishuddha

THE FISH – MATSYASANA

BENEFITS

❖ Improves posture.
❖ Deters wrinkles.
❖ Benefits the thyroid gland.
❖ Frees blocks in Vishuddha Chakra.

PRECAUTIONS

❖ Place a cushion under your head if
  you prefer.

1 Sit on the mat with your legs together, straight out in front of you. Lean back, placing one elbow on the mat, then the other.

2 Inhale, arching your back and lowering the crown of your head onto the floor. (Use a cushion if this strains your neck too much.) Hold the posture for a few moments, breathing quietly. Make the affirmation: *I trust my inner voice, and speak the truth clearly.*

3 If you are comfortable taking it to the next stage, arch your back further, taking your elbows off the mat and resting your hands on your thighs or holding them in prayer position on your chest. Your body is now supported by the crown of your head and the buttocks. Hold for a count of ten if you are comfortable, breathing quietly.

4 Slide your head along the mat and stretch out fully to finish. Counterpose by lifting your head up off the mat and looking at your feet. Relax.

ajna the brow chakra

ajna = to perceive or to know

Location
Slightly above and between the eyebrows, projecting forward.

Purpose
This powerful center controls our ability to see from a deeper level, and governs intuition; it is often referred to as the third eye. As speech is to the throat center, so vision is to the brow center – this is the realm of the "seer," the wise one who, guided by an inner teacher, has wisdom beyond the norm. It increases the powers of visualization and spirituality.

Color
Indigo blue, sometimes with a hint of yellow or violet.

Element
There is no earthly element associated with this chakra, but it can be associated with light.

Sense
All senses may be associated, but especially extrasensory perception.

Symbol
A two-petaled lotus on either side of a circle with a downward-pointing triangle within, and inside that the Om symbol. The petals represent wings of transcendence, or the two snake heads of Ida and Pingala, conjoining the male and female principle.

Age
Not applicable to this chakra.

Physical connections
Eyes, base of skull, face, nose, sinuses, cerebellum, and the central nervous system.

Gland
Most say pituitary, but a connection with the pineal has also been demonstrated.

Astrological connections
Neptune Ruled by Neptune, for its association with inner truths, imagination, and devotion.
Mercury For control of the intellect.
Sagittarius/Jupiter Holistic teachings and connections with expanded inner truths.
Aquarius/Uranus Divine inspiration and flashes of intuition.
Pisces/Neptune Imagination, intuition, and insight through devotion.

Sound
Any music that expands and opens the mind, more usually classical.

Vowel
"E" as in "easy," sung in the key of A.

Mantra
OM

Gemstones
Amethyst, purple apatite, azurite, calcite, sapphire, fluorite, lapis lazuli, opal.

Aromatherapy oils
Hyacinth, violet, rose geranium, jasmine, vetiver, basil, patchouli, rosemary, mint.

Balanced energy in Ajna
We have an understanding beyond the norm, a sense of the harmony in the world, and a deep spirituality. Introspection is part of our lives and we have flashes of

intuition – those eureka moments when we absolutely know the mystical truth of a situation. These intuitions come from a higher source and are absolutely reliable. They are not related to the material planes.

In most people inspiration from this center comes only in flashes, the occasional transient experience, and it develops only as a constant underlying awareness with long-term regular meditational, yogic, or spiritual practice. The clairvoyant (clear seer) or psychic has exceptional power in this center, and sometimes can use it for distant healing.

Unbalanced or blocked energy in Ajna

In a person with a blockage or imbalance in this chakra, we may see a person locked into the world of the intellect, the rationalist who has become top-heavy in that field, to the point of intellectual arrogance. There is little or no reflection, and life is full of material desires, with the rejection of spirituality, leading to feelings of isolation from the world, of emptiness.

Physically there may be nightmares, headaches, learning difficulties, poor vision, neurological disturbances, and glaucoma.

Suggested imbalances in Ajna through the nine Enneagram types

One   When striving for perfection on the material plane, placing emphasis on the rational to the detriment of the spiritual. Harsh self-judgment, denying spiritual guidance.

Two   In the Two's striving for acceptance, spending time in action "doing" rather than "being," allowing little time for positive introspection.

Three   When the emphasis is purely on the material, no reflection, action rather than "being" – much as the Two.

Four   When there is too much focus on image and competition to the detriment of spirituality. Also when the emotions are amped up and the ability to reflect is abandoned.

Five   The top-heavy weighting of intellect, allowing rationalization to take precedence.

Six   Fear blocking trust in the true nature of things, over-valuing the intellectual.

Seven   Constant action leading to a neglect of reflection. A superficiality when too many things are attempted at the same time.

Eight   Another active type who may fail to prioritize quiet, reflective time.

Nine   When they neglect their own spiritual needs in favor of that of others; being drawn off course from their own deeper agenda. Or when caught in introspection, churning things around.

Suggestions for balancing Ajna

- Take time alone, sitting quietly and reflecting.
- Look at the starry night sky.
- Become conscious of your intuitions by recording them in a special notebook. Note their effect, accuracy, and timing.
- Notice when coincidences happen, and record these.
- Chant "E" in the key of A, or repeat the mantra OM.
- Touch a drop of one of the associated oils on your forehead when you meditate.
- Wear indigo blue or gaze at one of the associated gemstones.
- Run your hands through a patch of mint and take the smell in deeply.
- Regularly use Ajna energy by asking for guidance from your higher self, and trust the answers you get.
- Keep up a regular daily practice of meditation.

Meditation

1 Sit in your comfortable meditation position, and focus on quiet breathing for a few minutes.

2 When you are deeply relaxed, inhale, contracting the muscles of the perineum (in the area of the Root Chakra, Muladhara), and feel as if you are drawing energy from there up to the Ajna Chakra.

3 With the out-breath, relax the muscles of the perineum and imagine that you are radiating indigo light out from Ajna Chakra.

4 Continue in this manner for several minutes. (You may feel warmth in the perineum or a tingling that may gradually spread to the brow.)

5 Come out of the meditation in the usual way, breathing quietly and listening to the sounds around you, and dedicate any insights you received to the greater good of mankind and creaturekind.

Pranayama exercise

ALTERNATE NOSTRIL BREATHING

1 Place the middle finger of your right hand on the Ajna Chakra and breathe in and out slowly through both nostrils. Breathe in to a count of five, and then hold for a count of five.

2 Now breathe in through both nostrils. Then close your right nostril with your thumb, and breathe out through the left nostril to a count of five.

3 Breathe in through the left nostril to a count of five, close it with your ring finger, release the thumb, and breathe out through the right nostril to a count of five, keeping your left nostril closed. Hold the breath out for a count of five.

4 Start the cycle again, breathing in through the right nostril, and keep the rhythm going for a few minutes, alternately breathing in and out through each nostril.

5 Relax your hand down to your lap, and breathe equally through both nostrils for a few minutes, enjoying the clear, cool feeling in your head.

6 End by repeating: *My mind is clear, I trust my intuition.*

BENEFITS

❖ Clears the head and nostrils.
❖ Balances right and left brain function.
❖ Activates the Ajna Chakra.

PRECAUTIONS

❖ Stop if you feel dizzy.
❖ Give your nose a good blow before you start.

sahasrara the crown chakra

sahasrara = thousandfold

Location
On the crown of the head, or slightly above, and projecting upward.

Purpose
Merging of the self with the universe to a point at which "I" and "you" disappear. Little is written about this chakra because only the truly enlightened may know it, and its qualities – said to include the brilliance of tens of millions of suns, the coolness of tens of millions of moons – are beyond imagination. When this chakra opens, awareness is expanded beyond description; there is vast, limitless knowledge beyond words or intellect. The realization of emptiness is considered to be enlightenment. Often incorrectly interpreted in a nihilistic way, this alludes to the realization of the ultimate nature of phenomena. This is an extremely difficult concept, and requires much wisdom and penetrative insight, and a life lived in devotion and ethical conduct.

Color
Violet, but also gold and white.

Element
Not applicable to this chakra.

Sense
Not applicable to this chakra.

Symbol
A thousand-petaled white lotus. The Om symbol.

Age
Not applicable to this chakra.

Physical connections
Cerebral cortex, brain, skin, and the whole body.

Gland
The pineal gland.

Astrological connections
Uranus Ruled by Uranus.
Capricorn/Saturn Inner focus, concentration on the Divine.
Pisces/Neptune Devotion, oneness with the Divine, dissolution of limits.

Sound
Silence.

Vowel
The Sanskrit "m," hummed in the key of B.

Mantra
Not applicable to this chakra.

Gemstones
Clear quartz, amethyst, diamond, white jade, white tourmaline, snowy quartz, herkimer diamond, alexandrite, sapphire.

Aromatherapy oils
Lavender, frankincense, rosewood, lotus, olibanum.

Balanced energy in Sahasrara
When energy is balanced in this chakra, the person is sensitive to their own and others' mental states. Physically they are healthy and have control over their emotions, and experience deeper connection with others. The mind is free from attachments and there are many insights. When action is taken, it is appropriate

and achieves the desired results. The connection between the mundane and the spiritual worlds is seamless, and psychic ability is strong. Free of mind, they exist in the world in a state of enlightenment – selfless, spiritual, and devoted.

Unbalanced or blocked energy in Sahasrara

A sense of alienation may prevail if there is unbalanced or blocked energy here; as well, there may be depression with obsessive thoughts. There may also be much confusion, selfish, egocentric behavior, and the inability to let go of anxieties and fear. Because of the inability to imagine cosmic unity, there is often an underlying feeling of dissatisfaction.

Physically, there may be over-sensitivity to pollution, chronic exhaustion, epilepsy, or Alzheimer's disease.

Suggested imbalance in Sahasrara through the nine Enneagram types

I don't feel comfortable hypothesizing specific effects for the nine types when energy is malfunctioning in this chakra. Please see above – Unbalanced or blocked energy in Sahasrara – to get an idea of how types may be affected.

Suggestions for balancing Sahasrara

- Make plenty of time in your life for silence.
- Live an ethical life, giving due consideration to others and to the planet.
- Meditate regularly, burning frankincense, or use one of the oils.
- Gaze at white lilies or at one of the associated gemstones.
- Release any limiting thoughts you may have.
- Spend time on a mountaintop, quietly observing the world around you.
- Spend time in nature.

Yoga posture to activate Sahasrara

THE HARE – SASANGASANA

The headstand is the usual posture recommended for this chakra. However, since many of us have necks incapable of taking that strain, and it is only for the experienced yogi and is best learned under the guidance of a teacher, I offer you the Hare as an excellent alternative.

BENEFITS

❖ Counters the force of gravity.
❖ Improves the complexion.
❖ Brings freshly oxygenated blood to the brain, pituitary, and thyroid glands.
❖ Activates Sahasrara.

PRECAUTIONS

❖ Never take your head below the heart if you have high blood pressure.
❖ Check first with your osteopath/doctor if you have a weak neck.
❖ Always take time to rest in the Child Pose for a few moments to finish.

1 On a mat on the floor, start this posture in the Child Pose.

2 Next, place your hands on the floor on either side of your knees. Inhale, lifting your buttocks up and transferring your weight to the crown of your head. Exhale.

3 Clasp your hands behind your back and raise them as high as you can, feeling the contraction between your shoulder blades. Breathe quietly, holding the pose for as long as is comfortable. Repeat the affirmation: *I open to the universe. There are no limitations.* Exhale back down to the Child Pose when you are ready to come out of the posture. Stay there for a few minutes, breathing quietly before you sit up.

Meditation/visualization

1 Sit in a comfortable, cross-legged position, straight back, neck lengthened, shoulders relaxed. Breathe quietly.

2 Visualize a violet light emanating from the crown of your head and projecting upward, the light growing brighter with each breath.

3 Now picture a white lotus flower in tight bud resting on the crown of your head.

4 As you continue to breathe quietly, visualize the lotus, in the radiance of the violet light, gradually opening a thousand petals until they fold open like a crown upon your head.

5 As you focus on the crown of petals, they begin to radiate golden light out into the universe. Stay with this light, connecting you to the universe, until you feel that you are ready to come out of the meditation.

Conclusion

I hope that you have enjoyed this journey with me through the layers of our being, from Enneagram type, through the elements and yoga postures, and how they affect the emotions, to the chakras. It is fitting that this book ends with the mystical Crown Chakra. I wish you delight and many insights on your journey through life – tread lightly, and know that you are not alone. At the very least you can trust that all the people of the same Enneagram type as you will share your struggles and understand exactly how you feel.

May you be well.
May you be happy.
May you be filled with loving kindness.

index

Acknowledgments

I would like to thank the following for their help, for the excellent feedback from the nine types, who checked that I had accurately reflected their points of view and who gave me their stories, and for technical and moral support:

Jo Godfrey Wood, Peggy Sadler, Jonathan Hilton, and Camilla Davis at Gaia; Elizabeth Haylett from the Society of Authors; Rosi Thomas, Howard Koolman, Tim Holland, Josephine Seccombe, Anne Binney, Renate Hering, Liz Stewart, Graham Paul, Brian Low, Isabel Perkins, Stella Barnes, Eric Salmon, Ebba From, Mary Masters, Jane Coerts, Michael Healy, Anna and Phil Butcher, Anne Gleeson, Ann Houghton, Louise Webster, Sarah and David Beanland, Nick and Maggie Kaye, Debby Leek, Colette Lyons, Maxine Christopher, Helena McEwen, Gill Edwards, Roy Whenary, Paul and Rosemary Cowan, Janet Swan, and Elisabeth Skinner. Last, but not least, my family – Owen Elias, Diana Van Meersbergen, Frank and Megan Elias-Bussink for their encouragement, and little Nina Bussink for making me splash in the puddles with her when it was all done.

Picture credits

Photographs on: p. 19 © Corbis/LWA - Stephen Welstead; p. 25 © Corbis/Philip Harvey; p. 31 © Getty Images/Taxi/ Sebastien Starr; p. 37 © Getty Images/Taxi /Peter Beavis; p. 43 © Corbis/George Shelley; p. 49 © Getty Images/ Image Bank/Romilly Lockyer; p. 55 © Corbis/Jon Feingersh; p. 61 © Corbis/Tom & Dee Ann McCarthy; p. 67 © Getty Images/Taxi/ Bruce Laurance.

For information on Mary's Enneagram and movement workshops and presentations, please contact *www.enneagramforthespirit.co.uk*

The publisher would like to thank Charlotte Medlicott (model).